DAILY WEALTH HABITS: YOUR 365-DAY FINANCIAL CHALLENGE

A Yearlong Guide for Beginners and Professionals to Build Wealth, Boost Financial Literacy, and Master Personal Finance in Minutes. The last Yearly Financial Planner you will ever need!

365 Day Challenge

Book 1

ALEX SUTTON

Contents

Introduction: Setting the Stage for Financial Success

Purpose of the Book

In a world where financial management can feel overwhelming and time-consuming, *Money Mastery in Minutes: A Yearlong Guide to Building Wealth, One Day at a Time* aims to simplify the journey. This book is designed for anyone seeking to take control of their financial future without sacrificing hours of their busy day. With just a few minutes each day, you can build a solid financial foundation that will empower you to make better decisions, grow your wealth, and achieve your financial goals.

The premise is simple: small, consistent actions lead to significant, lasting change. By breaking down complex financial concepts into manageable daily tips and challenges, you'll find that financial growth is not only achievable but sustainable. This daily approach ensures that by the end of the year, you'll have the knowledge, habits, and confidence to continue improving your financial health long after you've finished the book.

How to Use This Book

This book is organized into 365 bite-sized lessons and challenges, each designed to be completed in just a few minutes. Here's how to make the most of your journey:

- **Read Daily**: Start each day with a brief lesson. These insights range from budgeting tips and savings strategies to more advanced topics like investing and debt management.
- **Take Action**: Every day includes a small, actionable challenge that reinforces the lesson. Completing these tasks helps turn knowledge into practice and builds a habit of daily financial progress.
- **Track Your Progress**: Use a notebook or a digital tool to document your reflections, progress, and results as you complete each challenge. This habit will help you see how far you've come and maintain motivation.
- **Review Monthly**: At the end of each month, you'll find a goal-setting challenge to help you consolidate what you've learned and prepare for the upcoming month.

Whether you're a busy professional, a young adult just starting out, or someone seeking an easy-to-follow financial plan, this book is structured to fit seamlessly into your life. Each lesson is designed to be standalone, so don't worry if you miss a day—just pick up where you left off.

Assessing Your Starting Point

Before you dive into the daily lessons, it's important to take stock of where you currently stand financially. This brief self-assessment will help you understand your starting point and track your growth as you progress through the book.

Initial Self-Assessment

Take a few minutes to answer the following questions:

1. **Income and Expenses**:
   - Do you have a clear idea of your monthly income and expenses?
   - How often do you track your spending?
2. **Savings**:
   - Do you have an emergency fund? If so, how many months' worth of expenses does it cover?
   - Are you consistently saving a portion of your income?
3. **Debt**:
   - What types of debt do you currently have (e.g., credit cards, student loans, mortgage)?
   - Are you aware of the interest rates and repayment terms for each debt?
4. **Investments**:
   - Do you currently invest? If so, in what types of assets (e.g., stocks, bonds, mutual funds)?
   - Are you comfortable with the level of risk in your investment portfolio?
5. **Financial Goals**:
   - What are your short-term (within one year) and long-term (beyond five years) financial goals?
   - How confident are you in achieving them?

Documenting your answers to these questions will give you a baseline to measure your progress as you move through the year. By the end of this journey, you'll be able to revisit your self-assessment and see how far you've come.

Getting Started

Once you've completed the self-assessment, you're ready to dive into the daily lessons. Remember, the journey to financial mastery is not a sprint but a marathon. By dedicating just a few minutes each day, you are investing in your future and setting the stage for a lifetime of financial well-being.

Let's get started—your path to financial success begins today!

PART I
Basic Financial Literacy

BUILDING FINANCIAL AWARENESS: BASIC FINANCIAL LITERACY, UNDERSTANDING INCOME VS. EXPENSES, AND TRACKING SPENDING.

Building Financial Awareness: Basic financial literacy, understanding income vs. expenses, and tracking spending.

Day 1: The Importance of Financial Literacy

- **Lesson**: Financial literacy empowers you to make informed decisions that improve your financial well-being.
- **Task**: Start a spending log and write down every expense today.
- **Quick Insight**: "The journey of a thousand miles begins with one step." – Lao Tzu. Remember, knowing where you stand financially is that first, crucial step toward progress.

Day 2: What is Net Income?

- **Lesson**: Net income is what you earn after taxes and deductions. It's crucial for understanding how much money you have available.

- **Task**: Calculate your monthly net income and note it in your spending log.

Day 3: Gross Income vs. Net Income

- **Lesson**: Gross income is your total earnings before deductions. Understanding the difference helps with better budgeting.
- **Task**: Record any sources of gross income and associated deductions.

Day 4: Fixed vs. Variable Expenses

- **Lesson**: Fixed expenses remain constant (e.g., rent), while variable expenses change (e.g., groceries).
- **Task**: List your fixed expenses and track your variable expenses for today.

Day 5: The 50/30/20 Budget Rule

- **Lesson**: Allocate 50% of your income to needs, 30% to wants, and 20% to savings or debt repayment.
- **Task**: Categorize today's expenses using the 50/30/20 rule.

Day 6: Needs vs. Wants

- **Lesson**: Identifying needs (essential expenses) versus wants (non-essential) helps prioritize spending.
- **Task**: Highlight one expense from today and label it as a 'need' or 'want.'

Day 7: Why Tracking Expenses Matters

- **Lesson**: Tracking expenses uncovers spending habits and helps identify areas for improvement.

- **Task**: Review your expense log for the past week and note any patterns.

Day 8: Setting Financial Goals

- **Lesson**: Short- and long-term financial goals provide motivation and direction for spending and saving.
- **Task**: Write down one financial goal and assess how today's spending aligns with it.

Day 9: The Power of a Daily Spending Habit

- **Lesson**: Recording expenses daily ensures accuracy and keeps you aware of your spending.
- **Task**: Continue logging every expense, even small ones.

Day 10: Emergency Funds

- **Lesson**: An emergency fund can cover unexpected expenses and prevent debt accumulation.
- **Task**: Set a target amount for an emergency fund and record any contributions.

Day 11: Understanding Discretionary Spending

- **Lesson**: Discretionary spending covers non-essential items, often where budget cuts are easiest.
- **Task**: Identify one discretionary expense and consider reducing it.

Day 12: Tracking Spending Methods

- **Lesson**: Use apps or simple pen-and-paper methods to track expenses; consistency is key.
- **Task**: Experiment with a new expense-tracking method today.

Day 13: The Role of Receipts

- **Lesson**: Keeping receipts helps verify expenses and avoid underreporting.
- **Task**: Save receipts from today's purchases and add them to your log.

Day 14: The True Cost of Daily Habits

- **Lesson**: Small, recurring expenses (e.g., coffee) add up over time.
- **Task**: Calculate the monthly cost of one daily habit and record it.

Day 15: Weekly Expense Reviews

- **Lesson**: Reviewing your spending weekly allows for timely adjustments.
- **Task**: Review your expense log for the week and highlight any unnecessary purchases.

Day 16: Income vs. Expenses Check

- **Lesson**: Ensuring your expenses don't exceed your income is critical for financial stability.
- **Task**: Compare this week's total expenses to your income.

Day 17: The Hidden Cost of Fees

- **Lesson**: Bank fees and service charges can quietly drain your budget.
- **Task**: Review recent bank statements for hidden fees.

Day 18: Setting Daily Spending Limits

- **Lesson**: Daily spending limits help control variable expenses.
- **Task**: Set a reasonable spending cap for today and track if you stay under it.

Day 19: Cash vs. Card Spending

- **Lesson**: Paying with cash can make spending more tangible, potentially reducing unnecessary purchases.
- **Task**: Use cash for all purchases today and see how it affects your awareness.

Day 20: Reviewing Your Subscriptions

- **Lesson**: Monthly subscriptions can add up quickly without being noticed.
- **Task**: List your active subscriptions and their monthly costs.

Day 21: Keeping Your Receipts Organized

- **Lesson**: Organizing receipts helps track spending and simplifies budget adjustments.
- **Task**: Sort and organize this week's receipts.

Day 22: The Benefit of Round-Up Savings

- **Lesson**: Round-up savings programs help save small amounts with every purchase.
- **Task**: Look into apps that offer round-up savings and consider starting one.

Day 23: The Cost of Eating Out

- **Lesson**: Frequent dining out can quickly impact your budget.
- **Task**: Record today's food expenses and consider meal prepping as a lower-cost alternative.

Day 24: Planning for Irregular Expenses

- **Lesson**: Annual or semi-annual expenses need to be planned for to avoid budget disruptions.
- **Task**: Identify one upcoming irregular expense and start saving for it.

Day 25: Analyzing Last Month's Expenses

- **Lesson**: Reviewing past expenses reveals opportunities for budget adjustments.
- **Task**: Compare this month's spending to last month's and note changes.

Day 26: Creating a Buffer for Unexpected Costs

- **Lesson**: A buffer in your budget can cover unexpected minor expenses.
- **Task**: Set aside a small amount as a budget buffer and log it.

Day 27: Monitoring Spending Triggers

- **Lesson**: Identifying what prompts impulsive spending helps control it.
- **Task**: Reflect on any triggers that led to unplanned purchases today.

Day 28: Recording Even Small Expenses

- **Lesson**: Small expenses add up and should be tracked just like major purchases.
- **Task**: Note every small expense from today, no matter how insignificant it seems.

Day 29: Identifying Savings Opportunities

- **Lesson**: Finding small ways to save adds up over time.
- **Task**: Identify one cost-saving change you can make in your daily routine.

Day 30: Reflecting on the Month

- **Lesson**: Reflect on what you've learned and how your spending habits have changed.
- **Task**: Review your initial self-assessment and note improvements and insights.

Challenge: Create a Personal Budget and Identify Areas for Improvement

One of the most significant actions you can take toward financial stability is creating a personal budget. A budget is a comprehensive plan for managing your income, expenses, and savings. This month, the challenge is to craft a realistic budget based on your current income and spending habits and to identify areas where you can improve.

Steps to Create Your Personal Budget

1. **Track Your Current Spending**: Use your expense log from the daily lessons to review how much you've been spending over the past month.
2. **Categorize Expenses**: Divide your spending into categories such as housing, groceries, transportation, dining out, entertainment, savings, and discretionary spending.
3. **Compare Income and Expenses**: Calculate your total monthly net income and compare it with your total expenses.
4. **Set Budget Limits**: Assign realistic spending limits for each category. Ensure you allocate at least 20% of your income toward savings or debt repayment.
5. **Identify Areas for Adjustment**: Pinpoint categories where spending can be reduced, such as dining out or impulse purchases. Look for opportunities to redirect these funds into savings or essential expenses.

Tips for Budget Success

- **Be Honest**: Ensure your budget reflects your real income and expenses to avoid frustration.

- **Stay Flexible**: It's normal to adjust your budget as you learn more about your spending habits.
- **Use Budgeting Tools**: Apps or spreadsheets can simplify tracking and help automate calculations.

Goal: Establish a Habit of Daily Expense Tracking

The goal for Part 1 is to make daily expense tracking a consistent practice. This habit forms the backbone of your financial awareness and lays the groundwork for effective budgeting. By tracking expenses daily, you gain a clear, real-time view of where your money goes and can make informed adjustments as needed.

Why Daily Tracking is Essential

- **Improves Awareness**: You become more conscious of your spending choices.
- **Prevents Overspending**: Daily tracking helps prevent small expenses from adding up to significant costs.
- **Supports Budget Adherence**: When you know your daily expenditures, you're more likely to stay within your budget limits.

How to Build the Habit

1. **Choose Your Tracking Method**: Whether using a notebook, spreadsheet, or app, pick a method that fits your lifestyle.
2. **Set a Reminder**: Dedicate a few minutes at the end of each day to log your expenses.
3. **Review Weekly**: Take time each week to look at your tracked expenses and ensure they align with your budget.
4. **Stay Consistent**: Even if you skip a day, get back on track the next day. The goal is progress, not perfection.

By committing to this challenge and working towards the goal, you'll develop a strong foundation of financial awareness that will support your future financial goals.

PART II

Mastering the Art of Budgeting

BUDGETING TECHNIQUES

Day 31: What is Budgeting?

- **Lesson**: Budgeting is the practice of planning your income and expenses to manage your money efficiently. It ensures you have enough for essentials, savings, and discretionary spending.
- **Task**: Write down your current income and a rough estimate of your monthly expenses.

Day 32: The 50/30/20 Rule Overview

- **Lesson**: The 50/30/20 rule suggests allocating 50% of your income to needs, 30% to wants, and 20% to savings or debt repayment. This simple framework helps maintain balance.
- **Task**: Categorize your expenses from Day 31 using the 50/30/20 rule.

Day 33: Zero-Based Budgeting Explained

- **Lesson**: Zero-based budgeting involves assigning every dollar of income a job until you reach zero. It helps track where all your money goes.
- **Task**: Create a zero-based budget for this month using your current income.

Day 34: Creating Budget Categories

- **Lesson**: Break down your expenses into clear categories like housing, groceries, transportation, savings, and entertainment.
- **Task**: List out your categories and assign average amounts for each based on past spending.

Day 35: Fixed vs. Variable Expenses Review

- **Lesson**: Fixed expenses stay consistent (e.g., rent), while variable expenses change monthly (e.g., dining out). Differentiating these helps in budget planning.
- **Task**: Separate your expenses from the past week into fixed and variable categories.

Day 36: The Importance of Prioritizing Needs

- **Lesson**: Ensure your needs are covered first (housing, food, transportation) before allocating money to wants or savings.
- **Task**: Review your budget and ensure that needs are adequately funded.

Day 37: Tracking Expenses Daily

- **Lesson**: Daily tracking helps you see spending trends and adjust your budget in real time.
- **Task**: Continue tracking every expense today and reflect on any unexpected spending.

Day 38: Setting Realistic Spending Limits

- **Lesson**: Budgets need realistic limits. Review past expenses to set achievable spending caps for each category.
- **Task**: Adjust your category spending limits to be realistic based on last week's data.

Day 39: Budget Cushion for Unexpected Costs

- **Lesson**: Include a small buffer in your budget for unexpected expenses to avoid financial stress.
- **Task**: Add a "emergency buffer" line to your budget and allocate a small amount.

Day 40: Benefits of a Weekly Review

- **Lesson**: Reviewing your budget weekly allows you to make timely adjustments and stay on track.
- **Task**: Schedule a 15-minute block each week to review your budget and spending.

Day 41: Cash Envelope System

- **Lesson**: Allocate cash into envelopes for each category. Once the cash is gone, you're done spending in that category.
- **Task**: Try using the cash envelope system for one discretionary category this week.

Day 42: Importance of a Savings Goal

- **Lesson**: Allocating a set amount for savings each month helps build an emergency fund or achieve future goals.
- **Task**: Set a specific savings goal for this month and include it in your budget.

Day 43: Budgeting for Irregular Income

- **Lesson**: If you have fluctuating income, base your budget on your lowest expected earnings to avoid overspending.
- **Task**: Identify the lowest income month from the past year and plan your budget accordingly.

Day 44: Budget-Friendly Meal Planning

- **Lesson**: Meal planning reduces grocery costs and minimizes food waste, saving you money.
- **Task**: Plan your meals for the upcoming week and estimate grocery costs.

Day 45: Flexible Budgeting

- **Lesson**: Life changes; so should your budget. Adjust for unexpected events or changes in income.
- **Task**: Review your budget for areas that may need more flexibility and make adjustments.

Day 46: Budgeting Apps Overview

- **Lesson**: Apps like Mint, YNAB, and PocketGuard simplify budgeting by tracking expenses automatically.
- **Task**: Download and try using a budgeting app for tracking expenses this week.

Story 1: Budgeting Success with Tiffany Aliche (The Budgetnista)

Tiffany Aliche, known as "The Budgetnista," faced financial hardship but managed to pay off $35,000 in credit card *debt within two years by using disciplined budgeting techniques. She now teaches others how to take control of their finances through her workshops and books.*

Day 47: Budgeting for Fun

- **Lesson**: Allocate a small 'fun' fund to prevent feelings of deprivation and maintain balance.
- **Task**: Set aside a small amount for entertainment or hobbies in your budget.

Day 48: Importance of Emergency Savings

- **Lesson**: Budgeting for emergencies ensures you don't have to rely on credit in unexpected situations.
- **Task**: Add an emergency fund contribution to your budget, even if it's small.

Day 49: Debt Repayment Strategy

- **Lesson**: Prioritize high-interest debt for faster repayment and reduced overall interest.
- **Task**: Create a plan to pay extra toward the debt with the highest interest this month.

Day 50: Review Subscriptions Regularly

- **Lesson**: Review and adjust your budget to remove unused or unnecessary subscriptions.
- **Task**: Cancel at least one subscription you no longer need

Day 51: Budgeting for Seasonal Expenses

- **Lesson**: Plan for periodic expenses like holiday gifts or annual fees to avoid budget strain.
- **Task**: Add a line in your budget for upcoming seasonal expenses.

Day 52: How to Handle Budget Surplus

- **Lesson**: If you have extra money at the end of the month, allocate it to savings, debt, or future goals.
- **Task**: Identify a plan for any potential surplus in your budget.

Day 53: The Power of Round-Up Savings

- **Lesson**: Small, automatic round-ups on transactions can add up to significant savings over time.
- **Task**: Enable a round-up savings feature on your bank account if available.

Day 54: Reassessing Needs and Wants

- **Lesson**: Periodically review your budget to ensure your needs and wants align with your current priorities.
- **Task**: Reassess today's expenses and check if they align with true needs or wants.

Day 55: Budget Automation

- **Lesson**: Automate savings and bill payments to simplify your budget and ensure timely payments.
- **Task**: Set up automatic payments for one bill or an automated transfer to savings.

Day 56: Weekly Meal Prep for Savings

- **Lesson**: Prepping meals for the week cuts down on dining out and spontaneous grocery trips.
- **Task**: Prepare a meal plan for the next week and shop for ingredients within budget.

Day 57: Including Self-Care in Your Budget

- **Lesson**: Allocate funds for self-care to maintain mental and financial health.
- **Task**: Set aside a modest budget for a self-care activity this week.

Day 58: Budget Reflection Time

- **Lesson**: Dedicate time each month to reflect on your budget's effectiveness and make necessary changes.
- **Task**: Spend 15 minutes reviewing your budget progress this month.

Day 59: Importance of a Budget Journal

- **Lesson**: Keep a journal of budget insights and changes. It helps track what works and what doesn't.
- **Task**: Start a small budget journal entry summarizing key lessons learned this month.

Day 60: Long-Term Budget Planning

- **Lesson**: Plan budgets not just month-to-month but with an eye on long-term goals, such as retirement or major purchases.
- **Task**: Outline a long-term financial goal and steps needed to incorporate it into your budget.

Day 61: Celebrate Your Budget Wins

- **Lesson**: Celebrate milestones and small wins to keep motivated and reinforce positive budgeting habits.
- **Task**: Reward yourself within budget for maintaining consistent tracking and progress.

Challenge: Adjust and Perfect the Budget Created in Part 1

During part 1, you built the foundation of understanding your financial situation and created an initial budget. This part's's challenge is to refine that budget to better fit your real-life spending and income patterns. Here's how to approach this challenge:

1. **Review Your Initial Budget**: Take a close look at the budget you created last month. Identify areas where you overspent or underspent.
2. **Analyze Your Spending Data**: Use the data from your daily expense tracking to see if your spending aligns with your initial budget.
3. **Adjust Categories**: If certain budget categories need more or less allocation, adjust them to better reflect your spending habits.
4. **Include a Buffer**: Add a buffer for unexpected expenses if not already present.
5. **Incorporate Changes**: Adjust your budget based on lessons learned from the daily tasks, such as meal prepping, cutting subscriptions, or using the cash envelope system.

The goal of this challenge is to make your budget more accurate and adaptable, setting the stage for sustainable financial management.

Goal: Build a Sustainable and Realistic Monthly Budget

By the end of Part 2, your objective is to develop a monthly budget that is sustainable, realistic, and adaptable. A sustainable budget is one you can stick to over the long term without feeling overly restricted. It should balance your financial priorities, including:

- **Covering Needs First**: Ensure essentials such as housing, utilities, and food are fully funded.
- **Allocating for Savings and Debt**: Dedicate a portion of your income toward savings and debt repayment.
- **Allowing for Flexibility**: Life can be unpredictable, so build in some flexibility for unexpected costs.
- **Supporting Your Goals**: Make sure your budget aligns with your short-term and long-term financial goals, such as building an emergency fund or saving for a major purchase.

Achieving this goal means you will have a practical, customized budget that reflects your lifestyle, helps you manage your money confidently, and sets you on a path toward financial stability and success.

PART III
Cutting Costs and Boosting Savings

RUGAL LIVING TIPS, NEGOTIATING BILLS, AND FINDING WAYS TO SAVE WITHOUT SACRIFICING QUALITY OF LIFE.

Day 62: Embrace Meal Prepping

- **Tip**: Meal prepping saves time and money by reducing the need for takeout or last-minute grocery runs.
- **Task**: Plan and prepare meals for the next three days to save on dining costs.

Day 63: The Power of a Grocery List

- **Tip**: Sticking to a grocery list prevents impulse purchases and keeps spending in check.
- **Task**: Create a grocery list and shop with it, avoiding any off-list purchases.

Day 64: Utilize Coupons and Discounts

- **Tip**: Coupons, discount codes, and loyalty programs can significantly reduce costs on everyday items.
- **Task**: Find and use at least one coupon or discount code for your next purchase.

Day 65: Negotiate Your Bills

- **Tip**: Many service providers are open to negotiation, which can lower your bills.
- **Task**: Call one service provider (e.g., internet or phone) and negotiate for a better rate.
- **Quick Insight**: A real-world example is how tech entrepreneur Sara found she was spending $100 a month on unused subscriptions. Canceling these led to her saving over $1,200 a year.

Day 66: Embrace DIY Projects

- **Tip**: Doing simple home repairs or creative projects yourself can save money and be rewarding.
- **Task**: Identify one small repair or project you can DIY this week.

Day 67: Use Energy-Efficient Practices

- **Tip**: Lowering energy use by turning off lights, unplugging devices, and using energy-saving settings can reduce utility bills.
- **Task**: Implement three energy-saving practices today.

Day 68: Review Subscription Services

- **Tip**: Subscriptions can be sneaky expenses; cutting unused ones can save a lot.
- **Task**: Review all your subscriptions and cancel at least one that you don't use regularly.

Day 69: Limit Dining Out

- **Tip**: Eating out less frequently can save hundreds per month.

- **Task**: Commit to cooking all meals at home for the next three days.

Day 70: Buy Generic Brands

- **Tip**: Generic brands often offer the same quality as name brands but at a lower cost.
- **Task**: Choose generic brands for at least three items on your next shopping trip.

Day 71: Create a "No-Spend" Day

- **Tip**: Designating days where no money is spent can help reset spending habits.
- **Task**: Plan a no-spend day this week and prepare for it by ensuring essentials are covered.

Day 72: Use Cashback Apps

- **Tip**: Apps like Rakuten and Ibotta can help you earn cashback on purchases.
- **Task**: Download and use a cashback app for your next shopping trip.

Day 73: Sell Unused Items

- **Tip**: Selling items you no longer need can free up space and bring in extra cash.
- **Task**: Choose five items to sell online or at a local consignment store.

Day 74: Opt for Reusable Products

- **Tip**: Reusable products like water bottles and shopping bags save money over time compared to disposable ones.

- **Task**: Switch to using reusable items for one category (e.g., shopping bags).

Day 75: Use Public Transportation

- **Tip**: Public transit is often cheaper than driving, especially when considering gas, parking, and maintenance.
- **Task**: Use public transportation for one trip this week instead of driving.

Day 76: Plan Activities at Home

- **Tip**: Hosting movie nights or game nights at home is cheaper than going out.
- **Task**: Plan an at-home activity this weekend to avoid the cost of entertainment venues.

Day 77: Shop Second-Hand

- **Tip**: Thrift stores and second-hand shops offer quality items at lower prices.
- **Task**: Visit a thrift store and find one useful item for your home or wardrobe.

Day 78: Take Advantage of Free Events

- **Tip**: Community events, free concerts, and workshops provide entertainment without the cost.
- **Task**: Find and attend one free event in your area this week.

Day 79: Practice the 30-Day Rule

- **Tip**: Waiting 30 days before making non-essential purchases helps curb impulse buys.

- **Task**: Identify one item you want but don't need and commit to waiting 30 days before purchasing.

Day 80: Reduce Water Usage

- **Tip**: Shortening showers and fixing leaks can lower your water bill.
- **Task**: Implement at least two water-saving techniques today.

Day 81: DIY Cleaning Supplies

- **Tip**: Homemade cleaning supplies are cheaper and often eco-friendly.
- **Task**: Make one homemade cleaning product using common household items.

Day 82: Limit Coffee Shop Visits

- **Tip**: Brewing your own coffee saves significant money over time compared to buying it daily.
- **Task**: Commit to making your coffee at home for the next week.

Day 83: Avoid ATM Fees

- **Tip**: ATM fees add up quickly; use your bank's ATMs or get cashback at stores.
- **Task**: Plan your cash needs to avoid using out-of-network ATMs.

Day 84: Review Your Insurance Policies

- **Tip**: Reviewing and comparing insurance policies can reveal savings.

- **Task**: Call your insurance provider and inquire about discounts or bundle options.

Day 85: Use Your Library

- **Tip**: Libraries offer free access to books, movies, and sometimes tools or community events.
- **Task**: Visit your local library and borrow a book or movie.

Day 86: Repair Instead of Replace

- **Tip**: Fixing items instead of replacing them can save money and reduce waste.
- **Task**: Repair one item in your home that needs attention.

Day 87: Avoid Convenience Fees

- **Tip**: Some services add convenience fees for payments; plan to pay bills directly or in-person to avoid these.
- **Task**: Identify one bill with a convenience fee and pay it another way.

Day 88: Shop Sales Strategically

- **Tip**: Plan purchases around sales and clearance events to save money.
- **Task**: Plan your shopping for items that will go on sale this month.

Day 89: Utilize Free Online Resources

- **Tip**: Use free online learning resources for skill development instead of paying for courses.

- **Task**: Start one free course or watch a tutorial to learn a new skill.

Day 90: Meal Share with Friends

- **Tip**: Sharing meals with friends or hosting potlucks can lower food costs and build community.
- **Task**: Plan a potluck or meal share with friends this week.

Challenge: Reduce Expenses by 10% and Allocate Savings to an Emergency Fund

One of the key challenges in Part 3 is to identify opportunities to cut your current expenses by at least 10%. This can be achieved through various cost-saving strategies you've learned, such as meal prepping, negotiating bills, and reducing unnecessary spending. Once you achieve this reduction, allocate the savings directly to your emergency fund.

Steps to Achieve This Challenge

1. **Review Your Budget**: Go through your monthly expenses and identify categories where you can make cuts, like dining out, subscriptions, or utility costs.
2. **Track Savings**: Keep a log of how much you save each day and calculate the total at the end of the month.
3. **Direct Savings to Emergency Fund**: Ensure that the 10% you've saved is promptly moved to a dedicated emergency savings account to avoid spending it elsewhere.

This approach not only strengthens your budgeting skills but also provides you with a financial cushion for unexpected expenses.

Goal: Establish a $500 Emergency Fund or Grow an Existing One

The goal for Part 3 is to create or expand your emergency fund to at least $500. An emergency fund is crucial for handling unexpected costs like medical bills, car repairs, or urgent home maintenance without disrupting your budget or incurring debt.

Why This Goal Matters

- **Peace of Mind**: Knowing you have money set aside can reduce stress during financial emergencies.
- **Avoiding Debt**: An emergency fund prevents reliance on credit cards or loans when unplanned expenses arise.

Tips to Reach Your Goal

- **Automate Transfers**: Set up automatic transfers from your checking account to your emergency fund to make saving seamless.
- **Use Windfalls Wisely**: Allocate unexpected income like tax refunds or gifts to boost your emergency fund.
- **Stay Consistent**: Even if you can only save a small amount each week, consistency will help you reach your goal over time.

By the end of Part 3, you should have a clearer understanding of your expenses, effective cost-cutting strategies, and a solid start or boost to your emergency fund. This achievement sets the stage for greater financial security and prepares you for future parts focused on further financial growth.

PART IV

Strategic Debt Reduction

STRATEGIC DEBT REDUCTION: TYPES OF DEBT, INTEREST RATES, AND DEBT REPAYMENT STRATEGIES

Day 91: Understanding Types of Debt

- **Lesson**: Debts come in various forms such as credit card debt, personal loans, student loans, and mortgages. Understanding these types helps prioritize repayment.
- **Task**: List all your debts, including type, balance, and monthly payment.

Day 92: Secured vs. Unsecured Debt

- **Lesson**: Secured debt is backed by collateral (e.g., a car loan), while unsecured debt (e.g., credit cards) isn't. Unsecured debt often has higher interest rates.
- **Task**: Identify which of your debts are secured and which are unsecured.

Story 2: Emergency Fund Champion: Jamila Souffrant

Jamila Souffrant, founder of Journey to Launch, saved $85,000 in two years to build an emergency fund and achieve financial independence. Her story emphasizes the importance of building a safety net and how planning ahead can make a huge difference.

Day 93: Interest Rate Basics

- **Lesson**: The interest rate is the cost of borrowing money. Higher rates mean you pay more over time, so targeting high-interest debts first is crucial.
- **Task**: Record the interest rate for each debt you listed on Day 91.

Day 94: Fixed vs. Variable Interest Rates

- **Lesson**: Fixed rates remain the same throughout the loan term, while variable rates can fluctuate, impacting your payments.
- **Task**: Note which of your debts have fixed rates and which have variable rates.

Day 95: The Snowball Method Explained

- **Lesson**: The snowball method involves paying off the smallest debt first to build momentum, then moving to the next smallest.
- **Task**: Identify your smallest debt and create a plan to make extra payments toward it.

Day 96: The Avalanche Method Explained

- **Lesson**: The avalanche method focuses on paying off debts with the highest interest rate first, saving you more money in the long run.
- **Task**: Identify your debt with the highest interest rate and create a plan to pay it down.

Day 97: Comparing Snowball vs. Avalanche

- **Lesson**: The snowball method offers quick wins for motivation, while the avalanche method minimizes total interest paid.
- **Task**: Choose the method that aligns with your goals and write out why you selected it.

Day 98: Minimum Payments—A Trap to Avoid

- **Lesson**: Making only minimum payments extends repayment periods and increases the total interest paid.
- **Task**: Calculate how long it would take to pay off one debt if you only made minimum payments.

Day 99: Consolidation Loans

- **Lesson**: Debt consolidation combines multiple debts into one loan with a potentially lower interest rate, simplifying payments.
- **Task**: Research if debt consolidation could benefit your situation and note pros and cons.

Day 100: The Risks of Balance Transfers

- **Lesson**: Balance transfer offers can provide temporary relief but come with fees and require discipline to avoid more debt.

- **Task**: Review balance transfer options and consider if it could help with your highest-interest debt.

Day 101: Creating a Debt Repayment Plan

- **Lesson**: A structured repayment plan keeps you focused and consistent.
- **Task**: Draft a repayment schedule using either the snowball or avalanche method.

Day 102: Prioritizing High-Interest Debt

- **Lesson**: High-interest debts accumulate faster, so prioritizing them minimizes the total amount paid.
- **Task**: Re-examine your list of debts and ensure high-interest ones are prioritized.

Day 103: Setting Debt-Free Goals

- **Lesson**: Setting specific goals (e.g., "pay off $5,000 by next year") keeps you motivated.
- **Task**: Write down a debt-free goal with a timeline.

Day 104: Making Extra Payments

- **Lesson**: Extra payments can significantly reduce the loan term and total interest paid.
- **Task**: Plan an extra payment toward your highest-priority debt this month.

Day 105: The Snowball Effect on Motivation

- **Lesson**: The psychological boost of paying off smaller debts first can encourage you to keep going.
- **Task**: Plan how to celebrate when you pay off your first debt.

Story 3: Debt Reduction Journey: Mandy and Joe's Snowball Success.

Mandy and Joe, a couple featured in financial blogs, paid off $78,000 of combined student loans and credit card debt within three years by using the debt snowball method. They focused on paying the smallest debts first while maintaining minimum payments on larger debts, which gave them momentum and motivation.

Day 106: Avoiding New Debt

- **Lesson**: Reducing debt is only effective if you avoid taking on new debt.
- **Task**: Identify habits or triggers that lead to new debt and plan how to avoid them.

Day 107: Emergency Fund vs. Debt Repayment

- **Lesson**: Balancing debt repayment with emergency savings ensures you don't rely on credit during emergencies.
- **Task**: Allocate a small portion of your income to an emergency fund while continuing debt repayment.

Day 108: High-Interest Debt and Minimum Payments

- **Lesson**: Paying only the minimum on high-interest debt leads to prolonged repayment and high costs.
- **Task**: Identify one high-interest debt and plan to pay more than the minimum this month.

Day 109: The Impact of Late Payments

- **Lesson**: Late payments result in fees and can negatively affect your credit score.
- **Task**: Set up reminders or automatic payments to ensure timely payments.

Day 110: Snowball Method Success Stories

- **Lesson**: Many have successfully used the snowball method to pay off thousands in debt, thanks to early motivational wins.
- **Task**: Read or watch one story about someone who succeeded with the snowball method.

Day 111: Avalanche Method Success Stories

- **Lesson**: The avalanche method's focus on high-interest debt can save significant money on interest.
- **Task**: Research an example of someone who used the avalanche method effectively.

Day 112: Budgeting for Debt Repayment

- **Lesson**: Including debt repayment in your budget ensures you're allocating funds specifically for it.
- **Task**: Update your budget to include specific debt repayment amounts.

Day 113: Understanding APR (Annual Percentage Rate)

- **Lesson**: APR includes interest and fees, providing a clearer picture of total debt cost.
- **Task**: Review the APRs on your debts and note which have the highest costs.

Day 114: Debt Settlement Cautions

- **Lesson**: Debt settlement can reduce the principal owed but may damage your credit score.
- **Task**: Research if debt settlement is an option you should consider, but be cautious.

Day 115: Balance Transfer Fees

- **Lesson**: Balance transfers often come with fees, which can negate savings if not carefully considered.
- **Task**: Calculate if a balance transfer would save you money after fees.

Day 116: How Debt Affects Your Credit Score

- **Lesson**: High debt balances impact your credit utilization rate, a key factor in your credit score.
- **Task**: Check your credit score and see how your current debt may be impacting it.

Day 117: Celebrate Small Wins

- **Lesson**: Celebrating progress helps maintain motivation during long debt repayment journeys.
- **Task**: Plan a small, budget-friendly celebration for hitting your first repayment milestone.

Day 118: Refinancing Options

- **Lesson**: Refinancing can lower interest rates but comes with potential fees and extended loan terms.
- **Task**: Research if refinancing could lower your debt costs.

Day 119: Bi-Weekly Payment Strategy

- **Lesson**: Making bi-weekly payments instead of monthly can help pay down debt faster.
- **Task**: Set up bi-weekly payments for one of your debts.

Day 120: Debt Snowflake Strategy

- **Lesson**: Small, irregular extra payments (snowflakes) can make a big impact over time.
- **Task**: Use spare change or small windfalls to make an extra debt payment this week.

Day 121: Checking Your Debt Progress

- **Lesson**: Regularly checking your debt progress keeps you on track and motivated.
- **Task**: Review your debt repayment plan and assess your progress so far.

Challenge: Identify the Highest-Priority Debt and Create a Repayment Plan

In Part 4, the key challenge is to identify the debt that requires immediate attention—this could be the one with the highest interest rate, the smallest balance, or one that carries an emotional burden. Once identified, the next step is to create a structured repayment plan to tackle it effectively.

Steps to Complete This Challenge

1. **Evaluate Your Debt List**: Use the list of debts you compiled throughout Part 4, focusing on balances, interest rates, and types.
2. **Choose Your Priority**: Decide if you want to pay off the highest-interest debt first (avalanche method) or the smallest balance (snowball method).
3. **Develop a Plan**: Create a detailed plan with specific monthly payment amounts and timelines for your highest-priority debt.
4. **Set Milestones**: Break down your repayment into manageable milestones to keep track of your progress.

This challenge helps reinforce strategic debt reduction by narrowing your focus on a specific target and providing a clear action plan to follow.

Goal: Make an Extra Payment or Significantly Reduce One Debt

The ultimate goal of Part 4 is to make substantial progress on one specific debt. Whether it's by making an extra payment or significantly lowering the balance, this achievement will show the effectiveness of your repayment plan.

Why This Goal Matters

- **Reduces Total Interest**: Extra payments reduce the principal faster, which decreases the overall interest paid.
- **Boosts Momentum**: Seeing one debt reduced or paid off can motivate you to tackle the next one.
- **Builds Financial Confidence**: Successfully reducing a debt reinforces your capability to manage and eliminate your financial obligations.

Tips for Reaching This Goal

- **Use Windfalls Wisely**: Allocate any unexpected income, like bonuses or tax refunds, to make an extra payment.
- **Track Progress**: Regularly review your repayment milestones and adjust your strategy if needed.
- **Stay Disciplined**: Avoid taking on new debt while focusing on reducing your existing one.

By completing this challenge and reaching this goal, you will have taken a significant step toward overall debt reduction and financial freedom. It's a powerful move that will build both your confidence and your financial resilience.

PART V
Boosting Your Income

SIDE HUSTLES, MONETIZING SKILLS, AND NEGOTIATING SALARY

Day 122: Exploring Side Hustles

- **Lesson**: A side hustle can provide additional income without impacting your primary job. Options include freelancing, tutoring, or selling handmade products.
- **Task**: List three side hustles that interest you and research their potential earnings.

Day 123: Assess Your Skills

- **Lesson**: Identifying marketable skills is key to finding the right side hustle or monetizing what you already do well.
- **Task**: Write down your top five skills and brainstorm how you could use each to generate income.

Day 124: The Power of Freelancing

- **Lesson**: Freelancing platforms like Upwork and Fiverr

offer opportunities to monetize skills such as writing, design, or programming.
- **Task**: Create a profile on a freelancing platform and explore potential projects.

Day 125: Teaching and Tutoring

- **Lesson**: If you have expertise in a subject, teaching or tutoring can be a flexible way to earn extra money.
- **Task**: Identify a subject you could teach and research platforms or local opportunities for tutoring.

Quick Insight: "You don't have to be great to start, but you have to start to be great." - Zig Ziglar. Starting a side hustle may seem daunting, but each small step counts toward financial independence.

Day 126: Monetize Your Hobbies

- **Lesson**: Hobbies like photography, crafting, or baking can turn into profitable ventures.
- **Task**: Choose one hobby and outline steps to monetize it (e.g., selling photos online or at local markets).

Day 127: Selling Handmade Products

- **Lesson**: Platforms like Etsy make it easy to sell handmade or custom products.
- **Task**: List potential items you could create and sell, and research pricing strategies.

Day 128: Affiliate Marketing Basics

- **Lesson**: Affiliate marketing involves promoting products and earning a commission for each sale made through your referral.

- **Task**: Research affiliate programs related to your interests and sign up for one.

Day 129: Starting a Blog or Vlog

- **Lesson**: Blogging or vlogging can become a source of income through ads, sponsorships, and affiliate links.
- **Task**: Outline a content plan for a blog or vlog topic you're passionate about.

Day 130: Renting Out Space

- **Lesson**: Renting out a spare room or storage space can provide a steady stream of passive income.
- **Task**: Assess your home or property to see if you have space that could be rented out.

Day 131: Becoming a Virtual Assistant

- **Lesson**: Virtual assistants help businesses with tasks like email management, scheduling, and social media.
- **Task**: Identify potential clients or platforms to start offering virtual assistant services.

Day 132: Selling Digital Products

- **Lesson**: Digital products such as e-books, printables, or courses can provide passive income once created.
- **Task**: Brainstorm a digital product idea and outline steps to create it.

Day 133: Leveraging Online Marketplaces

- **Lesson**: Websites like eBay and Poshmark allow you to sell second-hand items or curated goods.
- **Task**: List five items in your home to sell and research how to price them competitively.

Day 134: Pet Sitting and Dog Walking

- **Lesson**: Pet services can be a rewarding way to earn extra cash, especially if you love animals.
- **Task**: Check local listings or apps for pet sitting and dog walking opportunities.

Day 135: Driving for Rideshare or Delivery Services

- **Lesson**: Services like Uber, Lyft, or DoorDash offer flexible income options.
- **Task**: Sign up for a rideshare or delivery service and complete the onboarding process.

Story 4: The Power of Side Hustles: Nick Loper

Nick Loper, founder of Side Hustle Nation, built multiple side hustles, including freelance writing and website building, that eventually replaced his 9-to-5 job income. His story shows that diversifying income streams can lead to financial freedom and flexibility.

Day 136: Monetize Your Art

- **Lesson**: If you have artistic talent, consider selling your art through galleries, online platforms, or commissions.
- **Task**: Create an online portfolio showcasing your work.

Day 137: Consulting and Coaching

- **Lesson**: If you have expertise in a field, consulting or coaching can be a high-paying side gig.
- **Task**: Define your niche and outline a plan to offer consulting services.

Day 138: Renting Out Equipment

- **Lesson**: Items like cameras, power tools, or camping gear can be rented out for extra income.
- **Task**: List valuable items you own that could be rented out and check rental platforms for opportunities.

Day 139: Starting a Small Business

- **Lesson**: Turning an idea into a small business can provide a sustainable income stream.
- **Task**: Write a one-page business plan outlining your idea, potential customers, and revenue model.

Day 140: Networking for Opportunities

- **Lesson**: Networking helps you discover side gigs and opportunities that align with your skills.
- **Task**: Reach out to at least three people in your network and share your availability for freelance work.

Day 141: Refining Your Resume

- **Lesson**: An updated resume that highlights skills relevant to side gigs or new roles can open doors.
- **Task**: Update your resume to emphasize skills that could attract side work or better job offers.

Day 142: Enhancing Your LinkedIn Profile

- **Lesson**: A well-crafted LinkedIn profile can attract clients and job opportunities.
- **Task**: Revamp your LinkedIn profile to showcase your skills and availability for freelance work.

Day 143: Participating in Paid Surveys and Focus Groups

- **Lesson**: While not high-paying, surveys and focus groups can provide quick, extra income.
- **Task**: Sign up for a legitimate survey site or focus group platform.

Day 144: Renting Out Your Car

- **Lesson**: Platforms like Turo allow you to rent out your car when it's not in use.
- **Task**: Check the requirements and feasibility of renting out your vehicle.

Day 145: Starting a Podcast

- **Lesson**: Podcasts can generate income through sponsorships and listener donations.
- **Task**: Plan the theme and structure of a podcast series you'd like to start.

Day 146: Selling Stock Photos

- **Lesson**: If you enjoy photography, selling stock photos online can create a passive income stream.
- **Task**: Take or select five quality photos and upload them to a stock photography site.

Day 147: Negotiating a Raise

- **Lesson**: Asking for a raise can boost your primary income. Prepare by researching industry standards and your achievements.
- **Task**: Prepare a list of accomplishments and schedule a meeting with your manager.

Day 148: Building a Side Hustle Schedule

- **Lesson**: Time management is key to balancing a side hustle with your main job.
- **Task**: Create a weekly schedule that allocates time for side work without burnout.

Day 149: Utilizing Passive Income Ideas

- **Lesson**: Passive income streams like investments or rental properties can supplement active earnings.
- **Task**: Research one passive income idea you could realistically pursue.

Day 150: Tracking Your Side Hustle Income

- **Lesson**: Keeping track of your side income helps you understand its impact and manage taxes.
- **Task**: Set up a simple spreadsheet or use an app to track all your side hustle earnings.

Challenge: Start a Small Side Project or Ask for a Raise

In Part 5, the main challenge is to take actionable steps to boost your income. This can be done by starting a small side project that aligns with your skills or interests or by approaching your employer to negotiate a raise. Both paths require planning, initiative, and confidence, but they can lead to substantial improvements in your financial situation.

Steps to Complete This Challenge

1. **Choose Your Path**: Decide whether you will start a new side project, such as freelancing, tutoring, or creating digital products, or if you will prepare to ask for a raise.
2. **Research and Plan**: For a side project, research the market, set realistic goals, and plan your initial steps. For a raise, prepare by documenting your recent achievements, understanding your value, and researching salary benchmarks.
3. **Take Action**: Launch your side project or schedule a conversation with your manager to discuss a raise.
4. **Track Progress**: Monitor your new income stream or salary change and make adjustments to improve your strategy.

Completing this challenge helps establish additional revenue that complements your primary income, providing more financial flexibility and security.

Goal: Increase Monthly Income by at Least 5-10%

The goal for Part 5 is to see a tangible increase in your monthly income by at least 5-10%. This increase can come from side work, a pay raise, or other revenue-generating activities. Reaching this target can have a meaningful impact on your financial health, allowing you to save more, pay down debt faster, or invest in your future.

Why This Goal Matters

- **Financial Security**: Additional income provides a cushion against unexpected expenses.
- **Faster Goal Achievement**: Extra earnings accelerate your progress toward savings, debt repayment, and other financial milestones.
- **Increased Confidence**: Successfully boosting your income reinforces your ability to adapt and grow financially.

Tips for Reaching This Goal

- **Stay Consistent**: Dedicate regular time each week to your side project or continue building skills to justify a raise.
- **Diversify Efforts**: If one side project doesn't yield the desired results, explore other options or add complementary income streams.
- **Evaluate and Adjust**: Periodically review your progress and refine your approach to maximize your income.

Achieving this goal sets a strong foundation for future financial growth and enhances your ability to manage both planned and unexpected financial needs.

PART VI

Investing 101

BASICS OF INVESTING, STOCKS, BONDS, MUTUAL FUNDS, AND INDEX FUNDS

Day 151: Understanding What Investing Is

- **Lesson**: Investing is the act of putting money into assets with the expectation of generating a profit or income over time.
- **Task**: Write down your current knowledge about investing and any questions you have.

Day 152: The Difference Between Saving and Investing

- **Lesson**: Saving keeps money safe for short-term needs, while investing aims for growth over the long term, usually with some level of risk.
- **Task**: Identify an amount of money you could allocate to investments rather than savings.

Day 153: Introduction to Stocks

- **Lesson**: Stocks represent ownership in a company.

When you buy shares, you become a part-owner of that company.
- **Task**: Research a well-known company's stock performance over the last year.

Quick Insight: Warren Buffett's success is a testament to the power of investing in stocks early and holding for the long term. "Someone is sitting in the shade today because someone planted a tree a long time ago." - Warren Buffett.

Day 154: What Are Bonds?

- **Lesson**: Bonds are essentially loans you give to governments or corporations in exchange for regular interest payments and the return of the principal at maturity.
- **Task**: Look up the current interest rates for government bonds and note their yield.

Day 155: Mutual Funds Explained

- **Lesson**: A mutual fund pools money from many investors to buy a diversified portfolio of stocks, bonds, or other securities managed by a professional.
- **Task**: Find and list one mutual fund that interests you and check its past performance.

Day 156: What Are Index Funds?

- **Lesson**: Index funds track a specific market index, like the S&P 500, offering broad market exposure with low fees.

- **Task**: Identify an index fund that tracks a major index and note its expense ratio.

Day 157: Benefits of Diversification

- **Lesson**: Diversification reduces risk by spreading investments across various assets to minimize the impact of poor performance in any one investment.
- **Task**: List at least three different asset types you would include in a diversified portfolio.

Day 158: Understanding Risk Tolerance

- **Lesson**: Risk tolerance is your ability and willingness to endure market volatility. It's essential to match your investments with your comfort level.
- **Task**: Take an online risk tolerance quiz to gauge your personal risk profile.

Day 159: Compound Interest Magic

- **Lesson**: Compound interest means earning interest on both your initial investment and the interest that accumulates over time, significantly growing your wealth.
- **Task**: Use an online compound interest calculator to see how a small investment grows over 10 years.

Day 160: Investing in Stocks vs. Bonds

- **Lesson**: Stocks typically offer higher returns but come with greater risk, while bonds provide more stability and lower returns.
- **Task**: Create a basic table comparing potential returns and risks of stocks and bonds.

Day 161: The Role of Dividends

- **Lesson**: Some stocks pay dividends, which are periodic payments made to shareholders from a company's earnings.
- **Task**: Research one dividend-paying stock and note its dividend yield.

Day 162: Understanding Market Volatility

- **Lesson**: Volatility refers to the frequency and magnitude of price movements in the market. Higher volatility means higher risk.
- **Task**: Check the volatility of a stock or index over the past month.

Day 163: The Importance of a Long-Term Perspective

- **Lesson**: Long-term investing helps weather short-term market fluctuations and takes advantage of compound growth.
- **Task**: Write down one long-term financial goal that investing could help you achieve.

Day 164: What Are ETFs (Exchange-Traded Funds)?

- **Lesson**: ETFs are similar to mutual funds but trade on exchanges like individual stocks, offering low fees and diversification.
- **Task**: Identify one ETF that aligns with your investment goals and note its main holdings.

Day 165: Dollar-Cost Averaging

- **Lesson**: Dollar-cost averaging involves regularly

investing a fixed amount, regardless of market conditions, which can reduce the impact of volatility.
- **Task**: Plan how you could start a dollar-cost averaging strategy with your current budget.

Story 5: Investing for Growth: Chris Reining

Chris Reining achieved financial independence by the age of 37 through diligent saving and strategic investing. He invested primarily in low-cost index funds and documented his journey, demonstrating that patience and disciplined investing can yield substantial financial freedom.

Day 166: Active vs. Passive Investing

- **Lesson**: Active investing involves handpicking investments to outperform the market, while passive investing tracks market indices.
- **Task**: Decide if you prefer active or passive investing and explain why.

Day 167: Understanding Investment Fees

- **Lesson**: Investment fees, such as expense ratios and transaction fees, can erode returns over time.
- **Task**: Compare the fees of two similar mutual funds or ETFs.

Day 168: Tax Implications of Investing

- **Lesson**: Investment gains can be taxed as short-term or long-term capital gains, with different rates depending on how long you hold an asset.

- **Task**: Learn the capital gains tax rate for your income bracket.

Day 169: The Role of an Emergency Fund Before Investing

- **Lesson**: Before investing, ensure you have an emergency fund to cover unexpected expenses so you don't need to liquidate investments early.
- **Task**: Confirm that you have at least three to six months of living expenses saved.

Day 170: Starting with a Brokerage Account

- **Lesson**: To invest in stocks, bonds, or funds, you'll need to open a brokerage account with an investment platform.
- **Task**: Research and compare two brokerage platforms for fees and ease of use.

Day 171: Analyzing Stock Performance

- **Lesson**: Analyzing stock performance involves looking at past trends, revenue growth, and market conditions.
- **Task**: Choose one stock and review its performance over the past year.

Day 172: Dividend Reinvestment Plans (DRIPs)

- **Lesson**: DRIPs allow you to automatically reinvest dividends to buy more shares, compounding your investment.
- **Task**: Find out if any stocks you're interested in offer a DRIP.

Day 173: Bonds vs. Bond Funds

- **Lesson**: Individual bonds pay a fixed interest until maturity, while bond funds pool various bonds to diversify risk.
- **Task**: List the pros and cons of investing in individual bonds versus bond funds.

Day 174: Index Fund Benefits

- **Lesson**: Index funds offer low-cost exposure to a broad market, making them a popular choice for new investors.
- **Task**: Research an index fund that has a strong historical performance.

Day 175: The 60/40 Portfolio

- **Lesson**: A traditional 60/40 portfolio consists of 60% stocks and 40% bonds, balancing growth and stability.
- **Task**: Create a simple 60/40 portfolio allocation for a hypothetical $1,000 investment.

Day 176: Investing in International Markets

- **Lesson**: Diversifying globally can reduce risk and increase potential returns by spreading investments across different economies.
- **Task**: Find one international ETF or mutual fund and review its top holdings.

Day 177: Understanding REITs (Real Estate Investment Trusts)

- **Lesson**: REITs allow you to invest in real estate without owning property, providing dividends and diversification.

- **Task**: Research one REIT and note its dividend yield and properties held.

Day 178: Staying Informed About Market Trends

- **Lesson**: Keeping up with financial news helps you make informed investment decisions.
- **Task**: Subscribe to a trusted financial news outlet or follow an investment podcast.

Day 179: Avoiding Common Investing Mistakes

- **Lesson**: Emotional decisions, chasing trends, and ignoring fees are common pitfalls that can impact your returns.
- **Task**: List three investing mistakes to avoid and plan how you will steer clear of them.

Day 180: Setting Up Automatic Investments

- **Lesson**: Automating investments ensures you stay consistent and removes the temptation to time the market.
- **Task**: Set up an automatic transfer from your bank to your brokerage account.

Challenge: Open an Investment Account and Make the First Investment

The challenge for Part 6 is to take actionable steps toward starting your investment journey. This involves opening an investment account and making your first investment, whether it's in stocks, bonds, mutual funds, or index funds.

Steps to Complete This Challenge

1. **Choose an Investment Platform**: Research and select a brokerage platform that aligns with your needs, such as low fees, user-friendly interfaces, or specific investment options.
2. **Set Up the Account**: Follow the platform's instructions to create an account, linking it to your bank for seamless transfers.
3. **Fund Your Account**: Transfer an initial amount to fund your account. This amount can be as small or large as you're comfortable with.
4. **Make Your First Investment**: Based on what you've learned, choose your first investment, whether it's an individual stock, a bond, a mutual fund, or an index fund.

Completing this challenge helps break the barrier to entry and builds confidence as you start seeing your money working for you in the market.

Goal: Create a Simple Investment Plan for Long-Term Growth

The goal for Part 6 is to design a straightforward investment plan that supports your long-term financial growth. This plan should outline your investment approach, including asset allocation, risk tolerance, and regular contributions.

Components of Your Investment Plan

- **Define Your Objectives**: Clearly state what you want to achieve with your investments, whether it's retirement savings, building wealth, or funding a major purchase.
- **Determine Asset Allocation**: Choose a mix of stocks, bonds, and other assets that align with your risk tolerance.
- **Set Up Regular Contributions**: Plan how much and how often you will contribute to your investments (e.g., monthly contributions).
- **Review and Adjust Periodically**: Commit to reviewing your portfolio periodically (e.g., annually) and making adjustments as needed to stay aligned with your goals.

Why This Goal Matters

- **Compounding Growth**: Starting an investment plan early maximizes the benefits of compound interest over time.
- **Financial Security**: A well-crafted plan can help secure your financial future and provide a safety net for unexpected expenses.
- **Confidence in Investing**: Following a structured plan builds your confidence and understanding of investment practices.

By reaching this goal, you establish a strong foundation for continuous financial growth, setting you on the path to achieving your long-term financial objectives.

PART VII
Smart Spending

NEEDS VS. WANTS, MINDFUL SPENDING HABITS, AND PRIORITIZING QUALITY OVER QUANTITY

Day 181: Understanding Needs vs. Wants

- **Lesson**: Needs are essential expenses for living (e.g., rent, groceries), while wants are non-essential (e.g., dining out, luxury items).
- **Task**: Review your last week's expenses and categorize them as needs or wants.

Day 182: Creating a Spending Hierarchy

- **Lesson**: Prioritize spending by ranking needs, wants, and savings goals to better manage finances.
- **Task**: Create a list ranking your typical expenses from most to least essential.

Day 183: The Benefits of Delayed Gratification

- **Lesson**: Delaying non-essential purchases helps determine if you truly want or need the item.

- **Task**: Choose one non-essential item you were planning to buy and delay the purchase for one week.

Day 184: Setting Spending Limits

- **Lesson**: Setting monthly limits for discretionary spending can prevent overspending.
- **Task**: Set a spending limit for one non-essential category and monitor your spending.

Day 185: Evaluating Subscriptions and Memberships

- **Lesson**: Review all subscriptions and memberships to ensure they add value.
- **Task**: Cancel at least one subscription or membership you don't use often.

Day 186: Prioritizing Quality Over Quantity

- **Lesson**: Investing in higher-quality items can save money in the long run as they last longer.
- **Task**: Identify one item you regularly buy that could be replaced with a higher-quality version.

Day 187: The 24-Hour Rule for Purchases

- **Lesson**: Waiting 24 hours before making a non-essential purchase helps prevent impulse buys.
- **Task**: Apply the 24-hour rule to any purchase you consider today.

Day 188: Tracking Your Impulse Purchases

- **Lesson**: Keeping track of impulse buys can help you identify spending patterns and triggers.

- **Task**: Document any unplanned purchases made this week and reflect on why you made them.

Day 189: Practicing Mindful Spending

- **Lesson**: Mindful spending means considering each purchase carefully to align with your values and goals.
- **Task**: For every purchase today, ask yourself if it aligns with your financial goals.

Day 190: The Importance of Budgeting for Fun

- **Lesson**: Allocating a specific amount for fun spending prevents feelings of restriction while maintaining budget control.
- **Task**: Set aside a small budget for a fun activity and plan when you'll use it.

Day 191: Reducing "Lifestyle Inflation"

- **Lesson**: Lifestyle inflation occurs when increased income leads to higher spending on wants rather than saving or investing.
- **Task**: Identify one recent change in your spending habits due to increased income and adjust it.

Day 192: Shopping with a Purpose

- **Lesson**: Shopping with a list and a purpose prevents unplanned purchases and saves money.
- **Task**: Write a list before your next shopping trip and stick to it.

Day 193: Considering Long-Term Value

- **Lesson**: Evaluate potential purchases based on their long-term value instead of immediate satisfaction.
- **Task**: For one item you plan to buy, consider how often you'll use it and its durability.

Day 194: Avoiding Buyer's Remorse

- **Lesson**: Buyer's remorse often stems from impulsive or unnecessary purchases.
- **Task**: Reflect on a recent purchase you regret and identify how to prevent future similar decisions.

Day 195: Practicing Gratitude

- **Lesson**: Appreciating what you already have can curb the desire for unnecessary spending.
- **Task**: List three non-monetary things you're grateful for today.

Day 196: Evaluating "Sale" Purchases

- **Lesson**: Sales can be tempting, but they're only worthwhile if the item is needed and valuable.
- **Task**: Before buying a sale item, ask if you would purchase it at full price.

Day 197: Setting Financial Priorities

- **Lesson**: Spending should align with your top financial priorities, such as savings, debt repayment, or major life goals.
- **Task**: Write down your top three financial priorities and check if your spending aligns with them.

Day 198: Reviewing Monthly Expenses

- **Lesson**: A monthly expense review helps ensure your spending aligns with your budget and financial goals.
- **Task**: Review your expenses for the past month and identify areas for improvement.

Day 199: Practicing Minimalism

- **Lesson**: Adopting a minimalist approach to spending can reduce clutter and increase savings.
- **Task**: Choose one area of your home to declutter and avoid buying replacements unless necessary.

Day 200: The Power of Saying "No"

- **Lesson**: Learning to say no to social events or activities that don't fit your budget helps maintain mindful spending.
- **Task**: Decline one unnecessary expense this week and reflect on how it feels.

Day 201: Comparing Quality Before Purchasing

- **Lesson**: Comparing product reviews and quality can help you choose items that last longer and save money over time.
- **Task**: Research reviews before making your next significant purchase.

Day 202: Reusing and Repurposing

- **Lesson**: Finding new uses for items you already own saves money and reduces waste.
- **Task**: Repurpose one item in your home instead of buying something new.

Day 203: Shopping Second-Hand

- **Lesson**: Buying second-hand items can save money and often provide good quality at a lower cost.
- **Task**: Visit a thrift store or browse an online marketplace for something you need.

Day 204: Avoiding "FOMO" Purchases

- **Lesson**: Fear of missing out (FOMO) can drive unnecessary spending on items or experiences.
- **Task**: Before making a purchase today, consider if it's motivated by FOMO.

Day 205: Embracing the "Budget-Friendly" Mindset

- **Lesson**: Adjusting your mindset to seek budget-friendly alternatives without sacrificing quality can lead to smarter spending habits.
- **Task**: Find a budget-friendly alternative to a purchase you've been considering.

Day 206: Avoiding Emotional Spending

- **Lesson**: Emotional spending often leads to regret. Recognize the emotional triggers that prompt unplanned spending.
- **Task**: Note how you're feeling before making any purchase today.

Day 207: Planning Purchases for Major Sales

- **Lesson**: Planning big purchases around major sale events can result in significant savings.
- **Task**: Create a list of items to buy during the next big sale event.

Day 208: Practicing Conscious Consumption

- **Lesson**: Conscious consumption involves considering the environmental and ethical impact of your purchases.
- **Task**: Research one product you regularly buy and explore eco-friendly alternatives.

Day 209: Celebrating Milestones Frugally

- **Lesson**: Celebrating doesn't have to break the bank; thoughtful, low-cost celebrations can be just as meaningful.
- **Task**: Plan a budget-friendly way to celebrate an upcoming milestone.

Day 210: Reviewing Your Smart Spending Progress

- **Lesson**: Reflecting on your spending changes and lessons learned helps reinforce good habits.
- **Task**: Write a summary of the most impactful changes you've made this month.

Challenge: Implement a No-Spend Week or a Limited Discretionary Spending Month

In Part 7, one of the key challenges is to put your mindful spending lessons into practice by attempting a no-spend week or limiting discretionary spending for an entire month. This challenge encourages you to become more aware of how much you spend on non-essential items and helps build stronger financial discipline.

Steps to Complete This Challenge

1. **Choose Your Approach**: Decide whether you want to attempt a no-spend week (where you only spend on essentials) or a month where you limit your discretionary spending.
2. **Set Clear Rules**: Define what counts as essential versus non-essential spending. For example, groceries and bills are essentials, while dining out and entertainment are discretionary.
3. **Plan Ahead**: Ensure you have everything you need for the no-spend week or prepare a strict budget for discretionary items if doing the month-long challenge.
4. **Track Your Progress**: Keep a log of your spending to ensure you're adhering to the rules you set.
5. **Reflect and Adjust**: After completing the challenge, reflect on what you learned and identify spending habits you can change permanently.

Completing this challenge helps you recognize spending patterns, curb impulse purchases, and find ways to redirect funds toward more meaningful goals, such as savings or debt repayment.

Goal: Refine Spending Habits for Better Financial Control

The goal of Part 7 is to refine your spending habits so that you have better control over your finances. This means prioritizing needs, choosing quality over quantity, and spending in ways that align with your long-term financial objectives.

Why This Goal Matters

- **Improved Budget Management**: Refined spending habits make it easier to stay within your budget and avoid financial stress.
- **Increased Savings Potential**: By cutting unnecessary expenses, you free up more money for savings or debt reduction.
- **Financial Mindfulness**: Being more conscious of where your money goes can lead to more thoughtful and fulfilling spending.

Tips for Achieving This Goal

- **Review Your Expenses Regularly**: Keep a close eye on your spending and make adjustments where needed.
- **Celebrate Small Wins**: Reward yourself (within budget) for achieving no-spend weeks or significant reductions in discretionary spending.
- **Adopt Sustainable Habits**: Integrate the lessons learned from this part into your everyday life for long-term financial health.

Achieving this goal helps lay a strong foundation for financial discipline, making it easier to pursue bigger goals like investing or debt elimination in the future.

PART VIII

Retirement Planning Basics

UNDERSTANDING 401(K)S, IRAS, AND COMPOUND INTEREST

Day 211: The Importance of Starting Early

- **Lesson**: Starting your retirement savings early takes advantage of compound interest, which grows your money exponentially over time.
- **Challenge**: Calculate how much you could save if you started investing $100 monthly starting today.

Day 212: What is a 401(k)?

- **Lesson**: A 401(k) is an employer-sponsored retirement plan that allows you to contribute pre-tax income, reducing your taxable income.
- **Challenge**: Check if your employer offers a 401(k) plan and review the contribution match, if available.

Day 213: Understanding IRAs (Individual Retirement Accounts)

- **Lesson**: An IRA is a retirement account you can set up independently, with tax advantages similar to a 401(k).
- **Challenge**: Research the differences between Traditional and Roth IRAs and decide which might be best for you.

Day 214: The Power of Compound Interest

- **Lesson**: Compound interest means earning interest on both your initial principal and the accumulated interest from previous periods.
- **Challenge**: Use an online compound interest calculator to see how much your retirement savings could grow over 20 years.

Day 215: Employer Match Explained

- **Lesson**: Many employers match a percentage of your 401(k) contributions, essentially giving you free money for retirement.
- **Challenge**: Determine if you're contributing enough to your 401(k) to receive the full employer match.
- **Quick Insight**: Financial advisor Jane Rodriguez once said, "If you're not taking advantage of your employer's 401(k) match, you're leaving free money on the table." Don't miss this valuable opportunity.

Day 216: Contribution Limits for 401(k)s

- **Lesson**: The IRS sets annual contribution limits for 401(k) accounts. For 2023, the limit is $22,500 for those under 50.

- **Challenge**: Check how much you're currently contributing and see if you can increase it within the limit.

Day 217: Roth vs. Traditional 401(k)

- **Lesson**: A Roth 401(k) is funded with after-tax dollars, so withdrawals in retirement are tax-free, while a traditional 401(k) is pre-tax but taxed upon withdrawal.
- **Challenge**: Assess which type of 401(k) aligns better with your expected tax situation in retirement.

Day 218: IRA Contribution Limits

- **Lesson**: For 2023, the IRA contribution limit is $6,500 for individuals under 50. Those 50 and older can contribute $7,500.
- **Challenge**: Check your current IRA contributions and plan to maximize them if possible.

Day 219: The Rule of 72

- **Lesson**: The Rule of 72 estimates how long it will take for your investment to double by dividing 72 by your annual rate of return.
- **Challenge**: Use the Rule of 72 to calculate how long it would take for your savings to double with your expected return.

Day 220: Diversifying Your Retirement Portfolio

- **Lesson**: Diversification helps reduce risk by spreading investments across different asset classes.
- **Challenge**: Review your retirement portfolio and ensure it includes a mix of stocks, bonds, and other investments.

Day 221: The Benefits of a Roth IRA

- **Lesson**: A Roth IRA allows for tax-free withdrawals in retirement, which can be beneficial if you expect to be in a higher tax bracket.
- **Challenge**: If you haven't yet, consider opening a Roth IRA and starting contributions.

Day 222: Tax Benefits of a Traditional IRA

- **Lesson**: Contributions to a traditional IRA may be tax-deductible, reducing your current taxable income.
- **Challenge**: Calculate how much you could save in taxes by contributing to a traditional IRA.

Day 223: Catch-Up Contributions

- **Lesson**: Individuals aged 50 or older can make catch-up contributions to their 401(k) or IRA, increasing their retirement savings.
- **Challenge**: If you're eligible, plan how you could make catch-up contributions.

Day 224: Understanding Vesting Periods

- **Lesson**: Some 401(k) employer contributions are subject to a vesting period, meaning you must stay with the company for a certain number of years to own them.
- **Challenge**: Review your 401(k) plan's vesting schedule.

Day 225: Penalties for Early Withdrawals

- **Lesson**: Withdrawing from a 401(k) or IRA before age 59½ often incurs a 10% penalty and taxes.
- **Challenge**: Write down alternative ways to handle

financial emergencies without tapping into retirement accounts.

Day 226: Required Minimum Distributions (RMDs)

- **Lesson**: Once you reach age 73, you must start taking minimum distributions from your traditional 401(k) and IRA.
- **Challenge**: Note the age at which you'll need to begin taking RMDs and plan for it in your retirement strategy.

Day 227: The Benefits of Starting Small

- **Lesson**: Even small contributions grow over time due to compound interest. Starting with what you can afford is better than not starting at all.
- **Challenge**: Increase your current contributions by $25-$50 if possible.

Day 228: Employer-Sponsored Plans Beyond 401(k)s

- **Lesson**: Some employers offer additional plans like 403(b)s or 457 plans, which also have tax benefits.
- **Challenge**: Check if your employer offers any plans beyond the 401(k) and explore their benefits.

Day 229: The Role of Index Funds in Retirement

- **Lesson**: Index funds offer low-cost exposure to the overall market, making them a popular choice for retirement accounts.
- **Challenge**: Review your investment choices and consider adding an index fund if you haven't already.

Day 230: Setting Retirement Savings Goals

- **Lesson**: Having a clear retirement savings goal helps you determine how much you need to save and invest.
- **Challenge**: Set a target amount for your retirement savings and create a timeline.

Day 231: Rebalancing Your Portfolio

- **Lesson**: Periodically rebalancing your portfolio helps maintain your desired asset allocation as investments grow at different rates.
- **Challenge**: Review your portfolio and make necessary adjustments to rebalance.

Day 232: Understanding Target-Date Funds

- **Lesson**: Target-date funds adjust the asset allocation automatically as you approach retirement age, becoming more conservative over time.
- **Challenge**: Research if a target-date fund aligns with your retirement plan.

Day 233: The 4% Withdrawal Rule

- **Lesson**: The 4% rule suggests that withdrawing 4% of your retirement portfolio annually can make your savings last for about 30 years.
- **Challenge**: Calculate what 4% of your projected retirement savings would be and see if it meets your needs.

Day 234: Social Security Basics

- **Lesson**: Social Security can supplement your retirement income, but it's best to not rely on it solely.

- **Challenge**: Estimate your Social Security benefits using the SSA's online calculator.

Day 235: The Importance of Low Fees

- **Lesson**: Investment fees can significantly reduce your retirement savings over time, so choosing low-fee options is crucial.
- **Challenge**: Review the fees on your current investments and look for lower-cost alternatives if needed.

Day 236: Roth Conversions

- **Lesson**: Converting a traditional IRA to a Roth IRA can offer future tax advantages, but comes with immediate tax implications.
- **Challenge**: Research if a Roth conversion would be beneficial for you.

Day 237: Understanding Annuities

- **Lesson**: Annuities can provide guaranteed income in retirement, but often come with high fees and complexity.
- **Challenge**: Learn about the different types of annuities and decide if they're worth considering.

Day 238: Keeping Beneficiaries Updated

- **Lesson**: Regularly updating the beneficiaries on your retirement accounts ensures your assets go to the intended recipients.
- **Challenge**: Review and update your beneficiaries as needed.

Day 239: Staying Informed About Retirement Changes

- **Lesson**: Legislation and tax laws can change, affecting retirement accounts and strategies.
- **Challenge**: Subscribe to a reliable financial news source to stay updated on changes.

Day 240: The Value of Professional Guidance

- **Lesson**: A financial advisor can help fine-tune your retirement strategy, especially as your financial situation becomes more complex.
- **Challenge**: Schedule a consultation with a financial advisor or attend a free consultation.

Challenge: Review or Start a Retirement Plan

The challenge for Part 8 is to either review your current retirement plan or, if you don't have one, take the first steps to create one. This review should include assessing your current contributions, understanding your investment choices, and ensuring your plan aligns with your long-term financial goals.

Steps to Complete This Challenge

1. **Review Current Contributions**: Check how much you are currently contributing to your 401(k), IRA, or other retirement accounts.
2. **Evaluate Investment Options**: Ensure your investments align with your risk tolerance and retirement timeline.
3. **Start a New Plan**: If you don't have a retirement account, research and open a 401(k) or IRA.
4. **Consult Resources**: Use tools or speak with a financial advisor to better understand your retirement strategy.

Completing this challenge sets you on the path to optimizing your retirement savings and ensuring your plan is comprehensive and effective.

Goal: Increase Retirement Contributions by 1-2% if Applicable

The goal for Part 8 is to boost your retirement contributions by 1-2%, if possible. Increasing your contributions, even slightly, can have a significant impact over the long term due to the power of compound interest.

Why This Goal Matters

- **Accelerates Savings Growth**: Even a small percentage increase can grow substantially over time.
- **Maximizes Employer Matching**: Ensures you are taking full advantage of any employer contribution matches.
- **Prepares for the Future**: A higher contribution rate helps you stay on track for a comfortable retirement.

Tips for Achieving This Goal

- **Automate Increases**: Set up automatic contribution increases if your retirement plan allows it.
- **Review Budget**: Look at your monthly budget to find areas where you can adjust to accommodate a higher contribution.
- **Start Small**: If 1-2% is too much at once, begin with a 0.5% increase and gradually build from there.

Reaching this goal enhances your retirement security and helps establish stronger financial habits that will benefit you in the long run.

PART IX
Advanced Investing Concepts

DIVERSIFICATION, RISK MANAGEMENT, AND PORTFOLIO BALANCING

Day 241: Understanding Diversification

- **Lesson**: Diversification means spreading your investments across different asset types to minimize risk.
- **Task**: Review your current investments and list the different asset classes you own.

Day 242: The Role of Asset Allocation

- **Lesson**: Asset allocation is the process of deciding how to divide your portfolio among various asset categories, such as stocks, bonds, and cash.
- **Task**: Assess your current asset allocation and compare it to your risk tolerance.

Day 243: Benefits of International Diversification

- **Lesson**: Investing in international assets helps protect your portfolio from domestic economic downturns.

- **Task**: Research one international fund or ETF to consider adding to your portfolio.

Day 244: Understanding Sector Diversification

- **Lesson**: Spreading investments across different sectors (e.g., technology, healthcare, finance) helps reduce the impact of underperformance in any single sector.
- **Task**: Identify which sectors your current investments are concentrated in and look for opportunities to diversify.

Day 245: Risk vs. Reward

- **Lesson**: Higher risk typically offers the potential for higher reward, but balancing risk is essential for long-term growth.
- **Task**: Evaluate one high-risk investment in your portfolio and decide if it aligns with your goals.

Day 246: Understanding Market Cycles

- **Lesson**: Markets go through cycles of growth (bull markets) and decline (bear markets). Knowing this helps you stay calm during downturns.
- **Task**: Review your investment timeline and determine how market cycles could impact your strategy.

Day 247: Correlation Between Assets

- **Lesson**: Correlation measures how different assets move in relation to each other. Low correlation can enhance diversification.
- **Task**: Research which of your assets have low or negative correlation.

Day 248: Balancing Growth and Stability

- **Lesson**: A balanced portfolio includes both growth (e.g., stocks) and stability (e.g., bonds) to weather market fluctuations.
- **Task**: Ensure your portfolio has a mix of growth and stability-focused investments.

Day 249: Rebalancing Your Portfolio

- **Lesson**: Rebalancing restores your portfolio to its original asset allocation, preventing unintended risk increases.
- **Task**: Check if your portfolio needs rebalancing based on recent performance.

Day 250: Dollar-Cost Averaging in Practice

- **Lesson**: Dollar-cost averaging involves investing a fixed amount regularly, reducing the impact of volatility.
- **Task**: Commit to a dollar-cost averaging strategy for one of your investments this month.

Day 251: The Importance of Bonds in Your Portfolio

- **Lesson**: Bonds provide income and reduce overall portfolio risk, acting as a stabilizing force.
- **Task**: Review your bond allocation and decide if you need to increase it for more stability.

Day 252: Defensive Investments

- **Lesson**: Defensive stocks, such as those in utilities and consumer staples, tend to perform better during market downturns.

- **Task**: Identify one defensive stock to consider adding for more balance.

Day 253: Understanding Volatility

- **Lesson**: Volatility refers to the degree of variation in investment prices. High volatility can mean higher potential gains but more risk.
- **Task**: Check the volatility of one of your current holdings using online financial tools.

Day 254: Evaluating Investment Fees

- **Lesson**: High fees can erode your returns over time, so choosing low-cost investments is vital.
- **Task**: Review the fees for your mutual funds or ETFs and consider switching to lower-cost alternatives if needed.

Day 255: Active vs. Passive Portfolio Management

- **Lesson**: Active management involves frequent trading to outperform the market, while passive management follows an index or strategy with minimal trading.
- **Task**: Decide if you prefer an active or passive approach for your portfolio and adjust accordingly.

Day 256: Hedging Against Risk

- **Lesson**: Hedging involves using financial instruments, like options or other assets, to offset potential losses.
- **Task**: Research one simple hedging strategy to protect part of your portfolio.

Day 257: Diversifying with Real Assets

- **Lesson**: Real assets, such as real estate or commodities, provide a hedge against inflation and diversify your portfolio.
- **Task**: Consider adding a real asset investment to your portfolio.

Day 258: The Benefits of Dividend-Paying Stocks

- **Lesson**: Dividend-paying stocks provide regular income and can be a stable addition to your portfolio.
- **Task**: Research one dividend-paying stock and evaluate if it fits your strategy.

Day 259: Portfolio Risk Management

- **Lesson**: Effective risk management involves understanding your portfolio's potential downsides and taking steps to mitigate them.
- **Task**: Identify the highest-risk asset in your portfolio and plan a strategy to manage that risk.

Day 260: The Role of Cash Reserves

- **Lesson**: Keeping a portion of your portfolio in cash helps take advantage of market opportunities and provides liquidity.
- **Task**: Assess if your cash reserve is adequate based on your investment goals.

Day 261: Importance of Reviewing Annual Returns

- **Lesson**: Regularly reviewing your annual returns helps you assess if your portfolio is meeting its performance goals.

- **Task**: Check your annual returns and compare them to your expectations.

Day 262: Tax-Efficient Investing

- **Lesson**: Strategies like investing in tax-advantaged accounts or choosing tax-efficient funds help minimize your tax burden.
- **Task**: Identify one tax-efficient investment strategy to implement.

Day 263: Sector Rotation Strategy

- **Lesson**: Sector rotation involves shifting investments between sectors based on the economic cycle to maximize returns.
- **Task**: Research which sectors perform best in the current economic phase and see if adjustments are needed.

Day 264: Evaluating Your Risk Tolerance Regularly

- **Lesson**: Your risk tolerance may change over time due to life events or market conditions.
- **Task**: Reassess your risk tolerance and ensure your portfolio reflects it.

Day 265: The Importance of Portfolio Reviews

- **Lesson**: Regular portfolio reviews help you stay aligned with your financial goals and adjust as needed.
- **Task**: Schedule a quarterly portfolio review to make necessary updates.

Day 266: Balancing Growth and Income Investments

- **Lesson**: Balancing growth stocks with income-generating investments ensures a steady cash flow and growth potential.
- **Task**: Review your portfolio for a healthy balance of growth and income-focused assets.

Day 267: Using Stop-Loss Orders

- **Lesson**: Stop-loss orders can protect your investments by automatically selling an asset when it reaches a certain price.
- **Task**: Set up a stop-loss order for one high-risk investment.

Day 268: The Role of Index Funds in Balancing

- **Lesson**: Index funds help maintain a balanced portfolio by providing exposure to a broad range of securities at a low cost.
- **Task**: Ensure you have exposure to at least one index fund in your portfolio.

Day 269: Benefits of Automated Portfolio Management

- **Lesson**: Automated tools or robo-advisors can help manage your portfolio efficiently and ensure it stays balanced.
- **Task**: Explore a robo-advisor service and consider using it for part of your portfolio.

Day 270: Reviewing Historical Data for Insights

- **Lesson**: Looking at historical performance data can

provide insights into how different assets perform under various conditions.

- **Task**: Review the historical performance of one asset you own.

Challenge: Rebalance Your Portfolio or Diversify Your Holdings

The challenge for Part 9 is to take actionable steps toward strengthening your investment portfolio. This involves rebalancing your portfolio to maintain your intended asset allocation or diversifying your holdings to reduce risk and enhance potential returns.

Steps to Complete This Challenge

1. **Review Current Allocation**: Assess your current portfolio to identify any over-concentration in certain asset classes or sectors.
2. **Rebalance if Necessary**: If your allocation has drifted due to market movements, make adjustments to bring it back in line with your goals.
3. **Add New Assets**: Explore new investment options to diversify, such as international stocks, bonds, or alternative assets.
4. **Monitor and Record**: Document the changes you make and monitor their impact over the next few months.

Completing this challenge helps ensure that your portfolio remains aligned with your investment strategy and risk tolerance.

Goal: Align Investments with Long-Term Financial Goals

The goal for Part 9 is to make sure your investment strategy supports your long-term financial aspirations. This means regularly reviewing and updating your portfolio to reflect any changes in your life circumstances or financial objectives.

Why This Goal Matters

- **Maintains Focus**: Aligning investments with your goals keeps your financial plan on track.
- **Optimizes Growth**: Regular adjustments help optimize your portfolio for both growth and risk management.
- **Adapts to Change**: Life changes, such as career shifts or major expenses, may require a portfolio reassessment to stay aligned with your priorities.

Tips for Achieving This Goal

- **Set Review Dates**: Schedule regular portfolio reviews (e.g., quarterly or annually).
- **Consult Experts**: Consider speaking with a financial advisor for deeper insights and personalized guidance.
- **Stay Educated**: Keep learning about new investment opportunities and strategies to continuously improve your approach.

Achieving this goal strengthens your financial plan, ensuring your investments are poised to support your long-term aspirations while managing risk effectively.

PART X
Protecting Your Wealth

INSURANCE TYPES, EMERGENCY PLANNING, AND FINANCIAL SECURITY

Day 271: The Importance of Emergency Funds

- **Lesson**: An emergency fund acts as a financial buffer for unexpected expenses, such as medical bills or car repairs.
- **Task**: Review your current savings and determine if you have at least three to six months of living expenses saved. If not, set a plan to build it.

Day 272: Understanding Health Insurance

- **Lesson**: Health insurance covers medical expenses and protects against high healthcare costs. It is essential for financial security.
- **Task**: Check your health insurance policy and review your coverage and benefits.

Day 273: Life Insurance Basics

- **Lesson**: Life insurance provides financial support to your dependents if you pass away, ensuring their financial stability.
- **Task**: Research different types of life insurance (term vs. whole life) and identify which might be suitable for your needs.

Day 274: Disability Insurance Explained

- **Lesson**: Disability insurance offers income protection if you are unable to work due to illness or injury.
- **Task**: Find out if your employer offers disability insurance or research private options.

Day 275: Homeowners/Renters Insurance

- **Lesson**: Homeowners or renters insurance covers property loss and liability, protecting your assets in case of damage or theft.
- **Task**: Review your current homeowners or renters insurance policy or explore new coverage if you don't have one.

Day 276: Auto Insurance Coverage

- **Lesson**: Auto insurance helps cover the cost of accidents, damages, or theft involving your vehicle.
- **Task**: Check your current auto insurance policy to ensure it provides adequate coverage.

Day 277: The Role of Umbrella Insurance

- **Lesson**: Umbrella insurance provides additional liability

coverage beyond standard insurance policies, protecting your assets from major claims.
- **Task**: Research whether umbrella insurance is suitable for your financial situation.

Day 278: Reviewing Insurance Deductibles

- **Lesson**: A deductible is the amount you pay out-of-pocket before insurance coverage kicks in. Choosing the right deductible balances premium costs and potential expenses.
- **Task**: Review your insurance deductibles and consider if adjustments are needed.

Quick Insight: Real-world advice: When James faced a major car accident, his well-reviewed insurance plan saved him thousands. Reviewing your policies can make a significant difference when it counts.

Day 279: Building a Will and Estate Plan

- **Lesson**: An estate plan ensures your assets are distributed according to your wishes and helps avoid legal complications for your beneficiaries.
- **Task**: Start drafting a simple will or explore estate planning services if you don't have one.

Day 280: Power of Attorney

- **Lesson**: Assigning a power of attorney allows someone to make financial or medical decisions on your behalf if you're unable to.
- **Task**: Consider assigning power of attorney to a trusted individual and review the necessary documentation.

Day 281: Understanding Health Savings Accounts (HSAs)

- **Lesson**: HSAs are tax-advantaged savings accounts for medical expenses and can be an effective part of your financial plan.
- **Task**: Check if you are eligible for an HSA and consider opening one to save on medical expenses.

Day 282: Emergency Planning Essentials

- **Lesson**: Having a comprehensive emergency plan, including important documents and contacts, helps manage crises more effectively.
- **Task**: Create or update an emergency folder with copies of essential documents and contact information.

Day 283: Cybersecurity and Identity Protection

- **Lesson**: Protecting your personal information online helps prevent identity theft and fraud.
- **Task**: Enable two-factor authentication on your important accounts and review your privacy settings.

Day 284: Reviewing Beneficiary Designations

- **Lesson**: Keeping beneficiary information updated ensures that your assets go to the intended recipients.
- **Task**: Check the beneficiaries on your insurance policies and retirement accounts and update them as needed.

Day 285: The Benefits of Long-Term Care Insurance

- **Lesson**: Long-term care insurance helps cover costs of extended care not typically covered by health insurance, such as assisted living.

- **Task**: Research long-term care insurance options and determine if it fits into your financial plan.

Day 286: The Importance of Regular Insurance Reviews

- **Lesson**: Periodically reviewing insurance policies ensures you have the right coverage and helps identify cost savings.
- **Task**: Schedule an annual review of all your insurance policies.

Day 287: Setting Up an Emergency Contact List

- **Lesson**: Having a designated list of emergency contacts ensures quick communication during a crisis.
- **Task**: Update your emergency contact list and share it with family members.

Day 288: Safeguarding Important Documents

- **Lesson**: Storing important documents, such as birth certificates and wills, in a secure location prevents loss and damage.
- **Task**: Ensure you have a safe or digital backup for essential documents.

Day 289: Understanding Credit Monitoring

- **Lesson**: Regular credit monitoring can help you detect fraudulent activity early and protect your financial standing.
- **Task**: Sign up for a credit monitoring service or use free tools to keep track of your credit.

Day 290: Planning for Natural Disasters

- **Lesson**: Preparing for natural disasters includes having a financial plan to cover unexpected costs and protect assets.
- **Task**: Make a checklist of items needed for a disaster emergency kit and ensure you have the funds available for sudden expenses.

Day 291: Reviewing Your Emergency Fund Periodically

- **Lesson**: Regularly assessing your emergency fund helps ensure it's sufficient for current living expenses.
- **Task**: Review your emergency fund and set a goal to increase it if needed.

Day 292: The Role of Trusts in Estate Planning

- **Lesson**: Trusts help manage assets during your lifetime and distribute them after your death, often with tax benefits.
- **Task**: Consult with an estate planner to see if setting up a trust is beneficial for your situation.

Day 293: Fraud Protection and Scams Awareness

- **Lesson**: Being aware of common scams and fraud tactics can protect your finances and identity.
- **Task**: Educate yourself on current scams and share information with loved ones.

Day 294: Evaluating Home Safety and Insurance Discounts

- **Lesson**: Improving home safety can lead to lower insurance premiums and better protection against theft or damage.

- **Task**: Install safety measures, such as smoke detectors or security cameras, and check for potential insurance discounts.

Day 295: Reviewing Insurance Riders

- **Lesson**: Riders are add-ons to insurance policies that provide additional coverage for specific needs.
- **Task**: Review your insurance policies to see if any riders are applicable to your coverage needs.

Day 296: Setting Up a Financial Backup Plan

- **Lesson**: A financial backup plan, such as a secondary income source or additional savings, helps maintain financial security during disruptions.
- **Task**: Identify one backup plan you can implement, such as a side hustle or secondary savings account.

Day 297: Emergency Fund Growth Strategies

- **Lesson**: Growing your emergency fund gradually helps maintain financial security and prepares you for larger unexpected expenses.
- **Task**: Automate a small portion of your paycheck to go directly into your emergency fund.

Day 298: Life Insurance Policy Review

- **Lesson**: Reviewing your life insurance policy ensures it still meets your needs as your life circumstances change.
- **Task**: Review your current life insurance policy and make any necessary updates.

Day 299: Estate Planning for Digital Assets

- **Lesson**: Including digital assets, such as online accounts and cryptocurrencies, in your estate plan helps protect them after your death.
- **Task**: Make a list of your digital assets and include instructions for accessing them in your estate plan.

Day 300: Keeping a Financial Safety Net for Dependents

- **Lesson**: Ensuring that your dependents are financially secure through insurance and estate planning provides peace of mind.
- **Task**: Confirm that your financial plan includes adequate protection for your dependents.

Challenge: Review Current Insurance Policies and Adjust if Necessary

The challenge for Part 10 is to review all of your current insurance policies, including health, life, auto, and homeowners/renters insurance, to ensure they provide adequate coverage. If you identify gaps or outdated policies, take steps to adjust them to meet your current needs.

Steps to Complete This Challenge

1. **Gather Your Policies**: Collect all current insurance policy documents.
2. **Assess Coverage Levels**: Review each policy to understand what is covered, the limits, and any exclusions.
3. **Identify Gaps**: Check if there are areas where coverage may be insufficient or missing entirely.
4. **Consult with Your Insurance Agent**: If needed, reach out to an insurance agent to discuss changes or updates to your policies.
5. **Make Adjustments**: Update your policies to ensure you have adequate coverage for your health, life, and assets.

Completing this challenge helps you stay protected against unexpected events and ensures peace of mind.

Goal: Ensure Adequate Coverage for Health, Life, and Assets

The goal for Part 10 is to confirm that your current insurance plans provide comprehensive coverage for your health, life, and valuable assets. Having the right insurance coverage helps mitigate financial risks and provides a safety net for you and your loved ones.

Why This Goal Matters

- **Financial Security**: Proper insurance coverage can prevent significant financial setbacks in case of unexpected events.
- **Peace of Mind**: Knowing that you and your assets are protected reduces stress.
- **Adaptability**: Ensuring your coverage matches your current life stage and financial situation allows you to stay prepared for the future.

Tips for Achieving This Goal

- **Regular Reviews**: Schedule annual or semi-annual reviews of your insurance coverage.
- **Stay Updated**: Keep informed about changes in insurance policies and coverage options.
- **Adjust as Needed**: Life changes such as marriage, having children, or purchasing a home may require adjustments to your coverage.

Reaching this goal will provide a strong foundation for financial protection, ensuring that you are well-prepared to handle any unexpected challenges that come your way.

PART XI

Financial Literacy Deep Dive

Understanding Financial News, Economic Indicators, and Key Financial Concepts

Day 301: Reading Financial News

- **Lesson**: Understanding financial news helps you make informed investment and budgeting decisions.
- **Task**: Subscribe to a reliable financial news source and read one article today. Note any key terms or concepts you don't understand.

Day 302: GDP (Gross Domestic Product)

- **Lesson**: GDP measures the total value of goods and services produced by a country and is a primary indicator of economic health.
- **Task**: Find and review the current GDP growth rate of your country.

Day 303: Inflation Basics

- **Lesson**: Inflation represents the rate at which the general level of prices for goods and services rises, eroding purchasing power.
- **Task**: Research the current inflation rate and note how it affects your daily expenses.

Day 304: Interest Rates and Their Impact

- **Lesson**: Central banks set interest rates to influence economic growth and inflation. High rates can slow down borrowing, while low rates encourage it.
- **Task**: Check the current interest rate set by your central bank and reflect on how it impacts your loans or savings.

Day 305: Unemployment Rate

- **Lesson**: The unemployment rate measures the percentage of the labor force that is jobless and actively seeking employment.
- **Task**: Find out your country's current unemployment rate and consider how it reflects the state of the economy.

Day 306: Stock Market Indices

- **Lesson**: Stock indices like the S&P 500 and Dow Jones measure the performance of a section of the stock market.
- **Task**: Review the latest changes in a major stock index and see how it correlates with economic news.

Day 307: Understanding Bonds

- **Lesson**: Bonds are fixed-income investments representing a loan made by an investor to a borrower, typically corporate or governmental.
- **Task**: Research one type of bond (e.g., government or corporate) and note its current interest rate.

Day 308: The Role of Central Banks

- **Lesson**: Central banks, like the Federal Reserve or European Central Bank, control monetary policy and influence the economy.
- **Task**: Read a recent statement or announcement from your central bank and summarize its main points.

Day 309: Consumer Confidence Index (CCI)

- **Lesson**: The CCI measures how optimistic consumers feel about their financial situation and the economy.
- **Task**: Look up the current Consumer Confidence Index and reflect on its potential impact on consumer spending.

Day 310: Exchange Rates and Currency Value

- **Lesson**: Exchange rates determine the value of one currency in terms of another, affecting international trade and travel.
- **Task**: Check the current exchange rate of your local currency against the U.S. dollar or another major currency.

Day 311: Economic Recessions

- **Lesson**: A recession is a significant decline in economic activity across the economy, lasting more than a few months.
- **Task**: Research the last recession your country faced and list two major causes.

Day 312: Understanding Credit Ratings

- **Lesson**: Credit ratings assess the creditworthiness of a borrower, impacting interest rates on loans and bonds.
- **Task**: Review the credit rating of your country and understand how it influences national borrowing costs.

Day 313: The Importance of Financial Statements

- **Lesson**: Financial statements like income statements, balance sheets, and cash flow statements provide insight into a company's financial health.
- **Task**: Choose one company and review its latest quarterly financial statement.

Day 314: The Role of Inflation in Investment

- **Lesson**: Inflation affects purchasing power and can erode investment returns over time.
- **Task**: Calculate the real return on an investment by subtracting the current inflation rate from its nominal return.

Day 315: Diversification and Risk Management

- **Lesson**: Diversifying investments helps mitigate risk by spreading funds across various assets.

- **Task**: Review your current investments and identify areas where you could diversify further.

Day 316: Understanding ETFs (Exchange-Traded Funds)

- **Lesson**: ETFs are investment funds traded on stock exchanges, combining the benefits of mutual funds and stock trading.
- **Task**: Research one ETF that interests you and review its holdings.

Day 317: The Importance of Liquidity

- **Lesson**: Liquidity refers to how easily an asset can be converted to cash without affecting its market price.
- **Task**: List the most liquid assets in your portfolio and those that are less liquid.

Day 318: Key Economic Indicators

- **Lesson**: Indicators such as GDP, unemployment rate, and inflation provide insights into economic trends.
- **Task**: Identify three key economic indicators and note their current values.

Day 319: Reading Annual Reports

- **Lesson**: An annual report provides comprehensive information on a company's financial condition and future prospects.
- **Task**: Select a company you follow and skim its latest annual report for strategic insights.

Day 320: The Basics of Supply and Demand

- **Lesson**: Supply and demand determine prices in a market; when demand exceeds supply, prices rise, and vice versa.
- **Task**: Observe a recent change in product prices and identify whether supply or demand drove the change.

Day 321: Understanding Dividends

- **Lesson**: Dividends are payments made by a company to its shareholders, usually derived from profits.
- **Task**: Find out if any of your investments pay dividends and check their yield.

Day 322: Bull vs. Bear Markets

- **Lesson**: A bull market indicates rising prices and investor confidence, while a bear market shows declining prices and pessimism.
- **Task**: Identify whether the current market is bullish or bearish and review its impact on your investments.

Day 323: The Role of Earnings Reports

- **Lesson**: Earnings reports detail a company's performance and influence stock prices based on results versus expectations.
- **Task**: Choose one recent earnings report and note its effect on the company's stock price.

Day 324: Understanding the P/E Ratio

- **Lesson**: The price-to-earnings (P/E) ratio helps investors determine if a stock is overvalued or undervalued relative to its earnings.

- **Task**: Calculate the P/E ratio of one stock you own or are interested in.

Day 325: Economic Moats and Competitive Advantage

- **Lesson**: An economic moat is a company's ability to maintain competitive advantages over its competitors.
- **Task**: Identify one company with a strong economic moat and explain why.

Day 326: The Role of Financial Advisors

- **Lesson**: Financial advisors offer expertise and tailored advice to help achieve financial goals.
- **Task**: Consider reaching out to a financial advisor for a consultation or review online resources for self-guidance.

Day 327: Reading Bond Yields

- **Lesson**: Bond yields indicate the return an investor can expect and are influenced by interest rates and credit risk.
- **Task**: Check the current yield of a government or corporate bond and compare it to historical averages.

Day 328: The Significance of Blue-Chip Stocks

- **Lesson**: Blue-chip stocks are shares in large, reputable, and financially stable companies, often paying reliable dividends.
- **Task**: Identify three blue-chip stocks and note their performance over the past year.

Day 329: Understanding Market Sentiment

- **Lesson**: Market sentiment reflects the overall attitude of investors toward a particular market or asset.
- **Task**: Read recent financial headlines and summarize the current market sentiment.

Day 330: The Importance of Personal Finance Education

- **Lesson**: Continuing to build your financial literacy helps you make informed decisions and adapt to economic changes.
- **Task**: Commit to reading one financial book or taking an online course to expand your knowledge.

Challenge: Read a Financial Book or Complete an Online Financial Literacy Course

The challenge for Part 11 is to take a proactive step to deepen your financial understanding by either reading a comprehensive financial book or completing an online course focused on financial literacy. This will reinforce what you've learned and expand your knowledge base.

Steps to Complete This Challenge

1. **Choose a Resource**: Select a financial book that covers investing, economic principles, or personal finance, or find a reputable online course.
2. **Set a Timeline**: Allocate time each day or week to read or complete course modules.
3. **Take Notes**: Document key takeaways and new concepts you learn for future reference.
4. **Apply Your Knowledge**: Identify areas in your financial life where you can implement what you've learned.

Completing this challenge equips you with deeper insights and practical knowledge for making informed financial decisions.

Goal: Improve Overall Financial Knowledge for Informed Decision-Making

The goal for Part 11 is to enhance your overall financial literacy to better understand market trends, economic indicators, and key financial principles. This knowledge empowers you to make sound financial choices that align with your long-term goals.

Why This Goal Matters

- **Confidence**: Greater financial literacy boosts confidence in managing and investing money.
- **Adaptability**: An informed mindset allows you to adjust your financial strategies as needed.
- **Better Outcomes**: Understanding complex financial concepts leads to more strategic and successful financial planning.

Tips for Achieving This Goal

- **Continuous Learning**: Commit to ongoing education, such as reading financial articles, watching educational videos, or attending workshops.
- **Stay Curious**: Regularly seek answers to financial questions that arise in your day-to-day life.
- **Discuss with Peers**: Share and discuss what you've learned with friends or mentors to reinforce your knowledge.

Achieving this goal ensures that you are well-equipped to navigate financial decisions with clarity and foresight, contributing to long-term financial stability and success.

PART XII

Reflection and Future Planning

Reviewing the Year's Progress, Revisiting Goals, and Setting New Objectives

Day 331: Reviewing Your Financial Journey

- **Lesson**: Reflecting on the past year's financial journey helps identify achievements and areas needing improvement.
- **Task**: List three major financial milestones you reached this year and three areas where you struggled.

Day 332: Assessing Goal Achievement

- **Lesson**: Revisiting your goals helps you understand which objectives you met and why.
- **Task**: Review the financial goals you set at the start of the year and note which ones you accomplished.

Day 333: Identifying Success Factors

- **Lesson**: Understanding what contributed to your financial successes can guide future strategies.
- **Task**: Write down the habits or actions that helped you achieve your financial goals.

Day 334: Learning from Challenges

- **Lesson**: Acknowledging challenges and setbacks allows you to learn and adapt.
- **Task**: Identify one financial challenge you faced this year and how you can improve moving forward.

Day 335: Evaluating Your Budget

- **Lesson**: Reviewing your budget helps ensure it still aligns with your financial situation and goals.
- **Task**: Compare your budget from the start of the year to your current budget and note any changes.

Day 336: Reassessing Spending Habits

- **Lesson**: Regularly analyzing spending habits can help you maintain financial discipline.
- **Task**: Review your last three months of spending and highlight areas for potential savings.

Day 337: Reflecting on Investments

- **Lesson**: Evaluating the performance of your investments helps you adjust your strategy for better results.
- **Task**: Review your investment portfolio's performance over the year and note any significant gains or losses.

Day 338: Emergency Fund Check-Up

- **Lesson**: Ensuring your emergency fund is sufficient provides financial security.
- **Task**: Verify the current balance of your emergency fund and set a goal for the upcoming year if needed.

Day 339: Celebrating Achievements

- **Lesson**: Recognizing and celebrating your financial achievements helps reinforce positive behaviors.
- **Task**: Choose one financial success from this year and celebrate it with a small, budget-friendly reward.

Day 340: Revisiting Long-Term Goals

- **Lesson**: Revisiting long-term goals ensures they still align with your future plans.
- **Task**: Review your long-term financial goals and make any necessary adjustments.

Day 341: Setting New Year Objectives

- **Lesson**: Setting clear financial objectives for the new year helps guide your financial plan.
- **Task**: Write down three main financial goals for the upcoming year.

Day 342: Prioritizing Goals

- **Lesson**: Prioritizing goals helps you focus on what's most important and allocate resources effectively.
- **Task**: Rank your financial goals from most to least important.

Day 343: Creating an Action Plan

- **Lesson**: An action plan turns goals into actionable steps.
- **Task**: Break down one of your new goals into actionable steps and set a timeline for each.

Day 344: Revisiting Savings Strategies

- **Lesson**: Adjusting savings strategies helps you stay on track to meet your goals.
- **Task**: Review your current savings plan and identify one area to enhance or change.

Day 345: Reviewing Investment Strategy

- **Lesson**: A yearly review of your investment strategy helps you align with changing market conditions and goals.
- **Task**: Consider if your current investment allocation still fits your financial goals for the upcoming year.

Day 346: Revisiting Insurance Needs

- **Lesson**: Your insurance needs may change over time, so reviewing them ensures you're adequately protected.
- **Task**: Review your insurance coverage and update policies if needed.

Day 347: Setting a Budget for the New Year

- **Lesson**: A well-thought-out budget sets the foundation for a financially successful year.
- **Task**: Create a preliminary budget for the first quarter of the new year.

Day 348: Planning for Major Life Events

- **Lesson**: Anticipating significant life events like moving, getting married, or having children helps you prepare financially.
- **Task**: List any major life events you expect next year and estimate their potential costs.

Day 349: Assessing Debt Reduction Progress

- **Lesson**: Reviewing how much debt you paid off over the year highlights your progress and guides next steps.
- **Task**: Calculate the total amount of debt reduced this year and plan for next year's payments.

Day 350: Reviewing Retirement Plan Contributions

- **Lesson**: Ensuring you're contributing enough to retirement accounts sets you up for long-term financial health.
- **Task**: Check your retirement contributions for the year and increase them if you can for next year.

Day 351: Creating a Financial Vision Board

- **Lesson**: A vision board visually represents your financial goals and helps maintain motivation.
- **Task**: Create a simple vision board or digital collage of your financial goals for the new year.

Day 352: Reviewing Financial Lessons Learned

- **Lesson**: Reflecting on what you've learned over the year helps you avoid past mistakes and replicate successes.
- **Task**: List three key financial lessons learned this year.

Day 353: Strengthening Financial Literacy

- **Lesson**: Continuous learning in financial literacy enhances decision-making skills.
- **Task**: Commit to one new financial learning resource for next year, such as a book or online course.

Day 354: Setting Quarterly Checkpoints

- **Lesson**: Quarterly checkpoints help you stay on track with your financial goals and make adjustments as needed.
- **Task**: Schedule quarterly check-ins to review your financial progress.

Day 355: Creating an Emergency Plan

- **Lesson**: Having an emergency plan in place ensures you're prepared for unexpected events.
- **Task**: Update or create an emergency plan, including contact lists and essential steps.

Day 356: Reviewing Your Financial Team

- **Lesson**: Having a solid financial team, such as advisors or accountants, can help manage complex financial needs.
- **Task**: Evaluate if you need to add any professionals to your financial team for the upcoming year.

Day 357: Setting Up Automatic Savings Adjustments

- **Lesson**: Automating savings helps ensure you consistently set aside money for future goals.
- **Task**: Adjust or set up an automatic savings increase for the new year.

Day 358: Planning for Tax Efficiency

- **Lesson**: Reviewing tax strategies helps you minimize liability and maximize deductions.
- **Task**: Review your tax deductions and plan any contributions or actions before the year ends.

Day 359: Goal-Setting Reflection

- **Lesson**: Reviewing your goal-setting process helps refine it for the future.
- **Task**: Reflect on which goals you achieved easily and which needed more effort, and adjust your approach for next year.

Day 360: Reviewing Your Financial Calendar

- **Lesson**: A financial calendar helps you keep track of important deadlines and financial obligations.
- **Task**: Create or update your financial calendar for next year with important dates like tax deadlines and payment reminders.

Day 361: Final Year-End Financial Reflection

- **Lesson**: A comprehensive review helps you close these 12 months with clear insights and prepares you for a strong start to the next 12 months.
- **Task**: Write a brief summary of your financial progress since you started with this book, including achievements and areas for improvement.

Day 362: Planning for Financial Growth

- **Lesson**: Identifying opportunities for financial growth helps you set goals that align with your future aspirations.

- **Task**: List three potential opportunities for growing your income or investments in the upcoming year.

Day 363: Reviewing Lifestyle and Spending Adjustments

- **Lesson**: Evaluating lifestyle choices and spending helps ensure they align with your overall financial goals.
- **Task**: Review your spending from the past year and note one lifestyle change that could help you save more.

Day 364: Setting Financial Priorities for the Next Year

- **Lesson**: Establishing clear financial priorities helps focus your efforts and resources where they matter most.
- **Task**: Write down your top three financial priorities for next year and create a brief action plan for each.

Day 365: A Day of Gratitude and Financial Reflection

- **Lesson**: Practicing gratitude can shift your mindset towards appreciating what you have accomplished and build motivation for future financial endeavors.
- **Task**: Take time today to reflect on the financial journey you've completed over the past year. Write a letter of gratitude to yourself, acknowledging your hard work, progress, and lessons learned. Identify one thing you are most grateful for regarding your financial progress and how it has impacted your life.

Quick Insight: "Reflect upon your present blessings— of which every man has many—not on your past misfortunes, of which all men have some." - Charles Dickens. Gratitude keeps you motivated to continue striving forward.

Challenge: Complete a Comprehensive Financial Review

The challenge for Part 12 is to conduct a thorough review of your financial year. This means assessing all aspects of your finances, including budgeting, savings, investments, debt management, and any financial milestones reached. This comprehensive review provides a clear understanding of your current financial state and highlights areas for improvement.

Steps to Complete This Challenge

1. **Gather Financial Documents**: Collect all relevant documents, such as bank statements, investment summaries, and expense reports.
2. **Review Each Financial Aspect**: Go through each category (e.g., savings, debt, investments) and assess its progress over the year.
3. **Identify Wins and Areas for Growth**: Note where you excelled and where adjustments are needed.
4. **Summarize Findings**: Write a summary of your financial year, including lessons learned and areas for focus.

Completing this challenge gives you a holistic view of your financial situation and sets a foundation for planning the next steps.

Goal: Create a Plan for the Next Year's Financial Growth

The goal for Part 12 is to develop a detailed financial plan for the next year that focuses on growth and sustainability. This plan should incorporate budgeting, investment strategies, debt repayment goals, and new savings targets to support your long-term financial objectives.

Why This Goal Matters

- **Provides Direction**: A clear plan guides your financial decisions throughout the year.
- **Enhances Growth**: By planning for growth, you increase your potential for achieving financial milestones.
- **Improves Financial Health**: Establishing a comprehensive plan helps manage risk and promotes better financial habits.

Tips for Achieving This Goal

- **Set SMART Goals**: Ensure your financial objectives are Specific, Measurable, Achievable, Relevant, and Time-bound.
- **Include Flexibility**: Allow for adjustments to your plan to account for unexpected changes.
- **Schedule Regular Reviews**: Plan quarterly check-ins to monitor progress and make necessary updates.

Reaching this goal ensures you start the new year with a structured approach, making it easier to pursue and achieve your financial ambitions.

Summary of Achievements: Review the Cumulative Progress of the Past Year

Congratulations on reaching the final chapter of **Money Mastery in Minutes**! Over the past year, you have dedicated yourself to learning and applying daily financial tips and challenges. This commitment, however small each step may have seemed, has created a strong foundation for your financial future. As you reflect on your journey, take pride in your progress and the discipline that has brought you here. Let's review the key milestones and achievements that have transformed your financial landscape over the past 12 months.

Month-by-Month Recap of Accomplishments

Part 1: Building Financial Awareness You began your journey by understanding your financial habits and assessing your current financial standing. By tracking daily expenses, you became more conscious of where your money goes and learned to identify patterns in your spending. This month established your baseline and equipped you with the insight needed to make informed decisions moving forward.

Part 2: Mastering the Art of Budgeting With a clear

understanding of your income and expenses, you dove into various budgeting techniques such as the 50/30/20 rule and zero-based budgeting. By the end of the month, you had fine-tuned a personal budget that balanced your needs and wants, setting a realistic blueprint for your monthly spending.

Part 3: Cutting Costs and Boosting Savings This part you embraced frugality and discovered ways to reduce costs without compromising your lifestyle. By negotiating bills, eliminating unnecessary subscriptions, and exploring cost-effective alternatives, you managed to cut your expenses by 10% and allocate the savings to your emergency fund. The goal of establishing or growing a $500 emergency fund became a reality.

Part 4: Strategic Debt Reduction Armed with knowledge about different types of debt and repayment strategies, you took significant steps toward reducing your financial obligations. Whether you used the snowball or avalanche method, you prioritized and tackled your debt with an actionable plan. Making an extra payment or significantly reducing one of your debts was a pivotal achievement, bringing you closer to financial freedom.

Part 5: Boosting Your Income Diversifying your income was the focus of **Part** 5. You explored potential side hustles, monetized your skills, or negotiated a raise at work. The month's challenge encouraged you to take proactive steps to increase your monthly earnings by 5-10%. This boost provided additional funds to invest, save, or expedite your debt repayment.

Part 6: Investing 101 With a stronger cash flow, you turned your attention to building wealth through investments. You learned the fundamentals of stocks, bonds, mutual funds, and index funds. By opening an investment account and making your first investment, you set the stage for long-term financial growth. This milestone marked your transition from saving to wealth-building.

Part 7: Smart Spending In Part 7, you honed your spending habits by distinguishing between needs and wants. Implementing mindful spending strategies, such as a no-spend week or limited discretionary spending, helped refine your approach to purchasing.

These exercises reinforced financial discipline and allowed you to focus your resources on what truly matters.

Part 8: Retirement Planning Basics You took a significant step toward securing your future by reviewing or initiating a retirement plan. By understanding 401(k)s, IRAs, and the power of compound interest, you developed strategies to enhance your long-term savings. Many readers successfully increased their retirement contributions by 1-2%, strengthening their future financial safety net.

Part 9: Advanced Investing Concepts Building on your foundational investing knowledge, you explored advanced topics such as diversification, risk management, and portfolio balancing. By rebalancing your portfolio or diversifying your holdings, you aligned your investments with your long-term goals, ensuring a well-rounded approach to financial growth.

Part 10: Protecting Your Wealth Month 10 shifted the focus to safeguarding what you had built. You learned the importance of insurance—health, life, home, and more—and emergency planning. Reviewing and adjusting your policies helped ensure you had adequate coverage and peace of mind, protecting your financial stability against unforeseen events.

Part 11: Financial Literacy Deep Dive You expanded your understanding by diving into more complex financial concepts and keeping abreast of economic indicators. By reading financial literature or taking an online course, you enriched your financial knowledge base. This deeper literacy empowered you to make well-informed financial decisions and engage more confidently in financial conversations.

Part 12: Reflection and Future Planning Finally, you reviewed your year's progress, evaluated your achievements, and celebrated your growth. Completing a comprehensive financial review set the stage for future success, allowing you to assess your strengths and identify areas for continued improvement. Setting new goals ensured that your momentum wouldn't stop at the close of this book but would carry forward into the next year and beyond.

Key Takeaways from Your Journey

1. **Daily Habits Matter**: Consistency in applying daily tips and challenges built lasting financial habits.
2. **Progress is Cumulative**: Small, incremental steps led to significant change over time.
3. **Adaptability and Growth**: Your ability to learn, adapt, and grow from each month's lessons positioned you to handle future financial opportunities and challenges confidently.
4. **Financial Confidence**: You've gained the knowledge and skills to make informed financial decisions, boosting your overall confidence in managing your money.

Long-Term Planning: Tips for Maintaining Financial Momentum and Setting Bigger Goals

As you celebrate your progress, it's essential to think about maintaining your financial momentum and setting bigger goals for the future. Here are some strategies to help you continue on your path to financial mastery:

1. Set New, Specific Goals Continue setting clear and measurable financial goals to keep yourself motivated. Whether it's saving for a down payment on a house, increasing your emergency fund to cover 6-12 months of expenses, or aiming for early retirement, new goals will help you stay focused.

2. Automate Your Finances Take advantage of automation to ensure consistency in saving, investing, and paying bills. Set up automatic transfers to your savings and investment accounts to build wealth without needing to think about it daily.

3. Review and Adjust Your Budget Regularly Your financial situation and priorities will change over time. Regularly review your budget and financial plan to adjust for new expenses, changes in income, or shifts in your goals. Flexibility is key to staying on track.

4. Continue Your Financial Education Stay informed about financial trends and strategies by reading finance books, attending workshops, or following reputable financial news sources. Ongoing education will keep your financial skills sharp and help you adapt to changes in the economic landscape.

5. Diversify Income Streams Explore additional ways to diversify your income, such as investing in rental properties, starting a small business, or exploring dividend-paying stocks. Multiple income streams can increase your financial security and accelerate your wealth-building efforts.

6. Revisit and Optimize Your Investments Periodically review your investment portfolio to ensure it aligns with your risk tolerance and long-term goals. Adjust asset allocations as needed to optimize for growth, stability, or income, depending on your stage in life.

7. Build and Maintain a Network Surround yourself with financially savvy individuals who can provide advice, motivation, or partnerships for new opportunities. Joining financial or professional groups can open doors to mentorships and resources that help propel your financial journey.

8. Plan for Life Changes Prepare for major life events, such as marriage, having children, or retirement, by updating your financial plan and savings strategy. Anticipating and budgeting for these transitions can help you navigate them with confidence.

9. Give Back Consider incorporating charitable giving into your financial plan. Supporting causes you care about not only benefits others but also fosters a sense of purpose and fulfillment, adding meaning to your financial success.

10. Stay Motivated and Celebrate Milestones Acknowledge and celebrate your financial achievements, whether big or small. Regularly take time to appreciate how far you've come and use those milestones as motivation to reach even higher goals.

Final Words

Your journey through this year-long guide has equipped you with the skills, knowledge, and mindset needed to manage your finances effectively and confidently. Embrace these lessons as life-long tools, and continue your path to financial independence with the same dedication that brought you through this book. Here's to your continued success and a future filled with financial mastery!

Resource Appendix: Additional Reading, Useful Tools, and Recommended Apps

To support your continued financial growth, here is a list of recommended books, tools, and apps that can help you maintain your momentum and expand your financial expertise:

1. Additional Reading

To continue expanding your financial knowledge beyond this guide, consider diving into the following highly recommended books and articles:

Books

- **"The Total Money Makeover" by Dave Ramsey**: A comprehensive guide on budgeting, saving, and debt elimination.
- **"Rich Dad Poor Dad" by Robert T. Kiyosaki**: Insights into the different approaches to wealth building and financial independence.
- **"Your Money or Your Life" by Vicki Robin and Joe Dominguez**: A step-by-step program on

transforming your relationship with money and achieving financial freedom.
- **"The Simple Path to Wealth" by JL Collins**: A straightforward guide to investing and building long-term wealth.
- **"The Millionaire Next Door" by Thomas J. Stanley and William D. Danko**: A study of the common habits of wealthy individuals that challenge stereotypes about millionaires.
- **"I Will Teach You to Be Rich" by Ramit Sethi**: A modern guide for young professionals on budgeting, investing, and enjoying life while growing wealth.

Articles and Websites

- **Investopedia**: Offers a wealth of articles covering financial concepts, investment strategies, and economic insights.
- **The Financial Diet (thefinancialdiet.com)**: A blog and online community focusing on financial literacy and lifestyle.
- **NerdWallet**: Comprehensive comparisons of financial products and practical advice for budgeting, investing, and credit management.
- **Mr. Money Mustache (mrmoneymustache.com)**: Engaging content on frugal living, early retirement, and financial independence.
- **The Balance (thebalance.com)**: A resource for clear, actionable financial advice and tips on saving, debt management, and investing.

2. Useful Tools

These tools will support you in staying on track, meeting your financial goals, and developing good money management habits.

Budgeting Tools

- **Mint (mint.com)**: A free budgeting tool that helps track your income, expenses, and financial goals all in one place.
- **YNAB (You Need A Budget)**: A paid tool that follows the principle of assigning every dollar a job to give you more control over your finances.
- **EveryDollar**: Created by Dave Ramsey's team, this app offers a zero-based budgeting approach to maximize financial awareness.

Investment Platforms

- **Vanguard**: Known for its low-cost index funds and investment accounts ideal for long-term, passive investing.
- **Fidelity**: Offers a range of retirement and investment accounts with comprehensive tools and zero-fee funds.
- **Robinhood**: A beginner-friendly app for trading stocks, ETFs, and cryptocurrency.
- **Acorns**: An app that rounds up your everyday purchases and invests the spare change, perfect for those new to investing.
- **M1 Finance**: Combines the benefits of robo-advisors and self-directed investing with fractional shares.

Debt Management Tools

- **Debt Payoff Planner**: A mobile app that helps create and visualize debt repayment plans, applying strategies like the snowball or avalanche method.
- **Undebt.it**: An online tool for mapping out debt repayment plans, prioritizing debts, and tracking your progress.
- **Credit Karma**: Monitors your credit score for free and

provides insights on credit card and loan offers tailored to your profile.

Savings and Expense Tracking

- **Qapital**: An app that automates savings through customizable rules (e.g., rounding up purchases or setting a 'guilty pleasure' savings trigger).
- **PocketGuard**: Simplifies budgeting by showing what's safe to spend after accounting for bills, goals, and necessities.
- **Simple (Banking app)**: Helps track your expenses and categorize spending in real-time.

Financial Literacy and Learning

- **Khan Academy's Personal Finance Series**: Free educational videos and exercises to learn about basic and advanced financial topics.
- **Coursera and Udemy**: Offer courses on personal finance, investing, and financial planning taught by experts.
- **Morning Brew's Money Scoop**: A free financial newsletter that breaks down complex topics into easy-to-digest insights.

3. Recommended Apps

Enhance your financial journey with these apps that make budgeting, investing, and saving easier and more engaging:

Budgeting and Tracking

- **Goodbudget**: A digital version of the envelope budgeting system, ideal for organizing your spending categories.

- **Spendee**: Customizable budget plans and shared wallets, great for households managing finances together.
- **Wally**: Offers detailed expense tracking and budget creation with multi-currency support.

Investment and Portfolio Management

- **Stash**: For beginners who want to learn about investing while building a diversified portfolio with as little as $5.
- **Wealthfront**: A robo-advisor with sophisticated financial planning tools and automated portfolio management.
- **Personal Capital**: Combines financial planning tools with investment tracking, ideal for understanding your net worth and long-term goals.

Savings Boosters

- **Digit**: An AI-driven app that analyzes your spending patterns and automatically saves small amounts for you.
- **Chime**: A banking app that includes features like automated savings and early direct deposit.
- **Honeydue**: Perfect for couples managing shared expenses, with tools to track bills, savings goals, and budgets.

Credit and Financial Health

- **Experian**: Monitor your credit score, understand what influences it, and receive tips on how to improve it.
- **Credit Sesame**: Offers a free credit score check and recommendations for improving your credit profile.
- **SoFi**: Provides tools for tracking credit, consolidating debt, and accessing financial advisory services.

4. Financial Planning and Professional Assistance

- **Financial Planning Services**:
  - **XY Planning Network**: A group of fee-only financial advisors who work with clients at all income levels.
  - **NAPFA (National Association of Personal Financial Advisors)**: Find certified, fee-only financial advisors who can provide unbiased advice.
- **Financial Calculators**:
  - **Bankrate's Calculators**: Cover everything from retirement savings to mortgage affordability.
  - **Investor.gov Compound Interest Calculator**: A helpful tool to see how your investments can grow over time.
  - **NerdWallet's Debt-to-Income Calculator**: Helps you understand your current debt load compared to your income.

This resource appendix is designed to keep you motivated and equipped with the best tools as you continue your journey towards financial mastery. Take advantage of these additional resources to deepen your understanding, make smarter decisions, and create a wealthier future one step at a time.

About the Author

Alex Sutton is a seasoned financial educator and personal finance coach with over a decade of experience helping individuals take control of their financial future. Known for his clear, approachable guidance, Alex has worked with diverse clients—from young professionals just starting out to established earners looking to refine their strategies. His practical, step-by-step approach has empowered many to build sustainable wealth and achieve their financial goals. Through workshops, speaking engagements, and now his book, Alex combines real-world insights with motivational storytelling to make financial mastery accessible and engaging for all.